Whitlock's Compositions

A Biographical and Pictorial Story of How
Charles D. Whitlock, Owner of Whitlock's Florist,
Attempted to Compose the Lives of His Two Daughters

Charlene Hampton Holloway, RN

The contents of this work, including, but not limited to, the accuracy of events, people, and places depicted; opinions expressed; permission to use previously published materials included; and any advice given or actions advocated are solely the responsibility of the author, who assumes all liability for said work and indemnifies the publisher against any claims stemming from publication of the work.

All Rights Reserved
Copyright © 2020 by Charlene Hampton Holloway, RN

No part of this book may be reproduced or transmitted, downloaded, distributed, reverse engineered, or stored in or introduced into any information storage and retrieval system, in any form or by any means, including photocopying and recording, whether electronic or mechanical, now known or hereinafter invented without permission in writing from the publisher.

Edited with assistance of Rebecca J. Holloway Hogan, Bachelor Communications, '92 Univ. Louisville, Lou., KY. Bonita Holloway Helm, Bachelor of Science, Sociology, '92 Univ. Louisville, Lou, KY Masters, Human Resources Management, '97 Webster Univ., St. Louis, Mo., C. Thelma Whitlock Hampton, Bachelor Public School Music, '39 Indiana University, Bloomington, IN, Mastrs, Science of Education, '62 Indiana Univeristy, Bloomington, IN. Francheska White, Jeffersonville, IN.

Cover Illustrations: Bruce Young, Louisville, KY
Cover Photography: Chester and Charlene Holloway, Louisville, Kentucky

Dorrance Publishing Co
585 Alpha Drive, Suite 103
Pittsburgh, PA 15238
Visit our website at *www.dorrancebookstore.com*

ISBN: 978-1-6491-3238-3
eISBN 978-1-6491-3717-3

This book is dedicated to:

My late great-great Grandmother, Cornelia Wallis (a former slave) owned by my late great-great Grandfather. My late Great-great Grandfather, Dr. John C. Whitlock, a Caucasian physician born in Virginia on March 18, 1818 who moved with both parents and paternal grandfather to Kentucky in 1830.

Dr. John C. Whitlock was published in an 1884 Chicago, IL-Louisville, KY article which stated he graduated from a Louisville medical school in 1842. He is also documented as a beginning student in an 1840 Louisville Medical Institute program with his noted preceptor, Dr. John A. Steele who is also published in the 1884 article of Dr. John C. Whitlock. Dr. Whitlock was also an 1846 elected official serving in the lower house of state legislature. My late great-grandparents, John and Hattie Whitlock and to all of their children: John Whitlock born before their union through John's first marriage and through their marriage: Solomon, Ellis, Detricth, Lillian, Dudley, Ethel and their youngest son, my late maternal grandfather, Charles Dade Whitlock and my late maternal grandmother, Parthenia Whitlock, his wife and Pal' of 59 years. All of my late great aunts and uncles. A special dedication to my mother's late sister, Mrs. Mildred Naomi Harris, R.N., who reached her potential to administer to thousands of people with various illnesses in many cities and several states. She encouraged her four children to reach their highest potential through the love and belief of God. A special dedication to my late father, Leon Henderson Hampton, Sr. who loved his daughter (pumpkin) and son, Leon Jr., unconditionally and stood proud when they accomplished many goals.

To my late paternal Grandmother, Loras Ellen Gray, who spent as much time as possible with her only granddaughter. To my dad's late sister, Gladora Tinsley, a true Christian wife of a minister and great mother to three sons and later in years, a daughter, Amber. A special dedication to my own late mother, C. Thelma Whitlock Hampton who I was able to watch the first 61 years of my life play the piano and organ in a grand manner and style for numerous church services, weddings, anniversaries, birthday parties, Vacation Bible School, state-wide and city-wide conferences of any faith. She played for numerous funerals and I saw her break down only one time while accompanying my late Dad as he sang for Mom's bosom-buddy friend, Mrs. Daisy Payne. Mom never compromised her gift of playing classical music, Negro Spirituals, Gospel music, hymns and songs of praise. She only stopped practicing and playing excerpts of G.F. Handel's Messiah with the perfection of not hitting a wrong note at the age of 84 years. Even up to the time of her death at age 91 years, Thelma continued at times to play for churches, high school graduation receptions, banquets for the Eastern Stars as well as regional meetings of the National Council of Negro Women.

A special dedication to Oprah Winfrey who encouraged me as one of her millions of viewers who have had the opportunity to follow her instructions. She has more than once encouraged people to look up their past and move forward with writing memoirs or books to encourage others.

A special dedication to Rev. Dr. Kevin W. Cosby, the senior pastor of St. Stephen Baptist Church who looked me in my eyes on a Sunday in June, 2004 and told me that I would indeed complete my book. Thanks for the prayers from everyone.

A special thanks to Rev. Ronald L. Gadson, pastor of Mt. Lebanon Baptist Church who helped me to understand and deal with the loss of my father in 1987 and who cheered me on to publish my book.

Special dedications to service women and men who have proudly defended our country in the past and those who continue to proudly serve our country in all of the branches of the U.S. armed forces. To those who have sustained critical and life-long injuries. This special dedication includes my late brother, a veteran of the U.S. Army, Leon H. Hampton, Jr. who passed away in Virginia with me by his side, September 30, 2010.

To all of God's people who profess their love for Him.

In Memory of My Late Father LEON HENDERSON HAMPTON, SR. Daddy, you never did mind staying in the background giving Momma, a Louisville 'Hometown Hero' the opportunity to play the piano or organ in a grand manner. She sometimes accompanied your melodious voice when you sang songs or praise. I thank our Heavenly Father for providing me with a one-in-a-million father who shared so much wisdom with his only daughter. When we all meet again, it will be one of the most wonderful family reunions.

This author, Charlene Hampton Holloway, R.N., forever grateful for the wonderful memories.

A Statement Offered
In Memory Of Our Grandfather

This is the end of a long and hard journey for our grandfather, having been reared in and around his home. We have been as close to our grandparents as we are to our own parents. And the love we feel in our hearts for them is as deep as the love that we hold for Thelma and Leon Sr.

We do not intend to eulogize our grandfather: We leave that task to the minister. But we felt it important to publicly state that although his frail body lies before us here, we know that this day he is in paradise with Jesus Christ and our beloved grandmother, Parthenia.

For more than thirty years, we watched the two of them fish, hunt, take trips, and work long hours together as a team—as Pals. They will be missed by a lot more people than just the immediate family because they gave of themselves so freely to all that they knew. Now they are re-united for eternity and we are happy for them. Because they loved the Lord with all their hearts and because they wanted to be together this way.

To some, unknowing, the death of Charles D. Whitlock will be but a notice in the morning newspaper, or a passing hearse on the street, but to those he worked with, his passing will surely mean more. He was a truly rugged individualist who, up until the time of his death, wanted only to make his own way in life: never content to sit on the sidelines and watch the world go by.

To others who knew him through the church, his passing will mean the end of an era where the fulfillment of his stewardship meant more than just tithing. It meant involving other families, especially children, in every phase of church activity. It meant that they could count on him to pick them up for church services. Pray for them when they were ill, bedridden, or troubled. Even give them money and food from his table when they were hungry. He took his stewardship seriously, and God will reward him for this.

To us, his grandchildren, he was simply Gramps who always reached into his pockets to let us have his change. He was our protector when we were wrong, our sponsor when education and family became important to us: our counselor when we sought advice. And all he ever really asked of us was to love him in return.

For this kind old gentleman, whose body and spirit were indeed weary of this life, we give thanks.

By Leon H. Hampton, Jr. and Charlene Hampton Holloway
May 7, 1981

Thanks to my Cheerleaders and Special Coach

My husband of 53 years, Chester (Chet) F. Holloway who has stood beside me spiritually to help me complete the dream of getting my book completed and published.

My late brother, Leon H. Hampton, Jr. who was a true 'Momma's Boy' who truly loved his sister, his nieces, nephew, grandnieces and nephews and cheered me on to reach my goal.

My three adult children, Becky, Bonnie and Chris who love their Mom and have been thankful for the main full-time babysitters, Charlene and Chet Holloway.

My six grandchildren, Janine D. Hogan (27 yrs.), Jonna K. Hogan (20 yrs.), daughters of Becky Hogan. Marcus D. Helm (27 yrs.), Maegan C. Helm (21 yrs.), son and daughter of Bonnie and Mark Helm. Christian S. Holloway, Jr. (21 yrs.), Chace W. Holloway (10 yrs.), sons of Christian S. Holloway, Sr. and Tiffany Ross Holloway.

My First cousins: the late Parthenia Mengstu, R.N. who as a brave warrior battled Multiple Sclerosis for twenty years who passed in December, 2007. Davida N. Harris, R.N., a dedicated Mom proud to have assisted her only child to graduate from Michigan State with a degree in Engineering.

Thelma L. Harris, R.N. who reached for the stars and wouldn't stop until she made straight A's obtaining her Master's Degree in Nursing. David F. Harris, Jr. who returned to San Antonio, Texas as a dedicated son to care for his ailing father suffering from a debilitating disease until he was called to glory.

To all of my Whitlock cousins, to include the late Mary Thelma Whitlock McCall, and all of the descendants of John and Hattie Whitlock. To my first and second cousins, the Tinsleys in Detroit, Michigan who have cheered me on. A special thanks to Albert Howard Burton, the youngest son of the Burtons who lived next door to my parents when I was a child and to his lovely wife, Beverly (native of Hopkinsville, KY) a great educator who continued to cheer me on to complete this book.

To the late Karen Kirby and her sister, Linda Alston for sharing their sisterly love.

To my Special Coach, Cathy Fyock, a great friend who has taken me under her wings to help my publication soar to great heights. I truly say thank you.

To everyone who has encouraged me to keep to the task to complete this book, my special thanks to you.

Encouraging Words

What a joy to have read Whitlock's Compositions. Charlene made the characters and the times come alive. This book, though unique to the Whitlock family, speaks out loud the saga of many African American families in this country.

Charlene's detailed account surely makes family members and friends proud to be connected by blood and by experience. Whitlock's Compositions affirms Charlene as the family griot and historian. I eagerly await the follow-up project. Well done Charlene. I know the next book will be just as rewarding as this one.

—Lesa Dae

Rev. Lesa Dae is one of the first ordained women ministers by senior pastor of St. Stephen Baptist Church, Rev. Dr. Kevin W. Cosby. St. Stephen Baptist Church's Louisville campus is located in the California Neighborhood at 1018 So. 15th Street, Louisville, Kentucky. With over 20,000 members, St. Stephen Baptist Church built over a decade ago a new Indiana campus, St. Stephen Baptist Church as well as providing ministries inside of Dosker Manor Housing on Muhammad Ali Blvd. St. Stephen Baptist Church in the past two years has established a church of many ministries as well in Elizabethtown, KY in Hardin County, Kentucky. Many great sermons have been delivered at all of these locations by women and men ministers from across America. Rev. Dr. Kevin W. Cosby is also President of Simmons College of Kentucky.

Rev. Lesa Dae is one of twelve children, obedient to the Word. She writes a weekly column in the Louisville Defender newspaper which is titled, "Be Encouraged". This newspaper like the daily Courier-Journal, Business First and even the Lexington Herald-Leader provides features and interviews of people of all cultures. The Louisville Defender newspaper has for a number of years hosted one of the largest Heritage Family Reunions in the country. It also featured Thelma Whitlock Hampton as a "Louisville Hometown Hero".

This author, Charlene Hampton Holloway, thanks Rev. Lesa Dae for all of her encouraging words as well as the fervent prayer she administered unto our Heavenly Father when she, Ms. Darnice Cloudy, Minister Angela Hasty, and Charlene sat together in Sunday School as Rev. Dae asked that this book be read all over the world. May one and all continue to praise His name all over the world.

Contents

Dedication		iii
In Memory of My Late Father LEON HENDERSON HAMPTON, SR.		v
A Statement Offered In Memory Of Our Grandfather		vii
Thanks to my Cheerleaders and Special Coach		ix
Encouraging Words		xi
Foreword		xv
Chapter 1	Charles D's childhood and birth parents	1
Chapter 2	The marriage of Charles D. Whitlock and Parthenia	5
Chapter 3	The births of Charles D. and Parthenia's daughters	9
Chapter 4	Charles D's STRICT RULES	13
Chapter 5	The Extension of the Whitlock love	17
Chapter 6	Thelma Enters Indiana University in Bloomington, Indiana	21
Chapter 7	Thelma's return from college and constant letters to Mildred	25
Chapter 8	The 'penny postcard' response	29
Chapter 9	Mildred's decision to marry a Methodist	35
Chapter 10	Thelma and Leon's first home they shared with Charlene	39
Chapter 11	Mildred and David move further away from Charles D	79
Chapter 12	Thelma's husband, Leon Sr. encourages her to teach many students piano	83
Chapter 13	Charles D's dependence upon family members to maintain the florist business	87

Chapter 14	Mildred continues to receive her special Entree'	.91
Chapter 15	Mildred and husband David increase their family	.95
Chapter 16	Spring trips to the Eastern part of the country	.99
Chapter 17	Mildred and husband David are blessed with their fourth child, a son	.103
Chapter 18	Reservations to the Holy Land	.109
Chapter 19	Two registered nurses graduate with pride	.115
Chapter 20	Charles D. loses his 'Pal' and soul mate but gains another registered nurse	.119
Chapter 21	Multiple losses of loved ones	.127
Chapter 22	Trying events in life—- but a Great Whitlock Reunion in 2004	.133
Bibliography		.141

Foreword

Statement made by Charlene Hampton Holloway's elementary, middle school, college roommate, and matron of honor.

"Whitlock's Compositions"

To my lifelong friend, Charlene Hampton Holloway.

This book has been your dream for many years and now it has come into fruition with a title that is so befitting of your grandfather's legacy. I thought of the word 'Composite' which is made up of distinct components which we are our family, friends and acquaintances that we come in contact over the course of our life time. In the case of your grandfather, a Florist, he developed a large plant family characterized by the Flower Head that being Charles Whitlock and his wife followed by their two daughters whose offspring became the more densely clustered flowers that appeared to be a single bloom called the Family.

From these components the Compositions spread in several directions leaving their mark and influence from Civil Rights, to Education, Nursing and the Legal arena.

Continue in the Word
Your Friend
Dorothy J. Letcher

Chapter 1

The late Charles D. Whitlock was born to the union of Hattie Morris and John Whitlock in the town of Hopkinsville, Kentucky, in 1898. He enjoyed having his oldest granddaughter, Charlene, listen to him relate to her about his early life. After all, Charlene was his namesake and she was born on his birthday, April 26th. Since Charlene's parents had no automobile at the time of her birth, Charles D. had driven his older daughter, Thelma, to the Louisville Red Cross Hospital for her second delivery. A late famous African American Louisville physician, Dr. Roscoe Bryant, performed the delivery of Charlene. Charles D. and Charlene were able to share specially made birthday cakes for 34 years. Charles D. worked at the main post office in Louisville, Kentucky, and he also owned a floral shop. Most often, Charles D. would sit on his work stool or stand while he busily designed his numerous floral arrangements and informed Charlene about his childhood as well as his young adulthood. Charles D. would speak very articulately and in a distinct manner to capture her full attention. At times, Charlene would walk into the floral workshop and hear Charles D. talking aloud when no one else was present. Charlene kidded with him about those times. He only laughed and said that he wanted to hear a great person speak. At times Charles D. was quite a jovial person. He spent many hours in his floral shop, which was an addition to his home. He and his wife, Parthenia, had proudly purchased their first home at 1611 West St. Catherine Street. That room addition was built with love by his good friend, Revered Luther Calvin. There were multitudes of flowers and designs from corsages, boutonnieres to casket sprays that had been carefully sculptured by Charles D. This artistic florist told Charlene that his mother, Hattie Morris Whitlock, died at the young age of 32 when he was only seven years old. His father, John Whitlock, became quite a lady's man soon after her death.

Charles D. had a bitter quiver in his voice when he spoke of John Whitlock. John and Hattie were parents to five sons: Solomon, Ellis, Dudley, Detricth, Charles D., and two daughters, Lillian and Ethel. Charles D. was the youngest son, but possessed a vivid memory of his mother and spoke highly of the love Hattie gave to him for the seven years he knew her.

Instead of speaking highly of his father, Charles D. often had many negative stories to tell Charlene such as how his father, bragged about being the son of a Caucasian doctor in Christian County, Kentucky. Charles D. said that John told him his father never took the opportunity to rear his son or even help put food on the table for his wife and seven children. Charles D. could not understand how a so-called family man had the audacity to brag about a father who admitted to a son's birth, but never supported him in any form or fashion. Charles D. told Charlene that John Whitlock was a very lightskinned colored man, with yellowish-colored eyes, who he reluctantly admitted was also a very handsome man. Because of his father's good looks, many women chased him even while he was married to his wife, Hattie. After Hattie died, many more women were pursuing John and at age seven, Charles D. was forced to find food to keep from starving. He was able to pick up lumps of coal strewn around the railroad tracks to sell then buy food for his older sister and brothers to cook for him and his baby sister, Ethel. Charles D. had a maternal uncle, named Charlie Morris. Charles D. was named after him. Uncle Charlie Morris was a very poor man struggling to maintain, but he lived a very quiet and long life. Years later, as a mature adult, Charles D. would take his wife, daughter, grandchildren, and in-laws to visit Uncle Charlie who quietly sat on his front porch at the ripe age of 110 years old. Even though Charles D.'s mother died at an early age, he had no idea longevity ran throughout his family genes. He did have enough insight, even at age seven, to know he had a very hard working mother raising seven children and trying to do domestic-type work outside her home. Charles D. stated that John Whitlock was a very conceited and selfish person who did not work very hard to care for his wife and family. As Charles D. grew up, he made up his mind early on that he would not be like his father. Charles D. was able to leave Hopkinsville, Kentucky, after working meager jobs to support himself.

Chapter 2

Little did Charles D. know that he had the potential of being a great poet and future entrepreneur in his lifetime. Charles D. was 16 years old when he moved to Louisville, Kentucky, following the footsteps of his oldest brother Solomon and older sister, Lillian. He was able to find meager jobs to become self-supportive. Charles D.'s father had settled down to marry a lady named Miss Melissa, whom he said was a very nice stepmother to him. In his mid-to late teens, he knew it was necessary to support himself.

Charles D. began to date a few girls, but one particular young lady, named Parthenia, caught his eye. After a short courtship, they married against the wishes of his older sister who constantly teased Charles D. about the dark skin of his wife. After thinking back about what his mother went through and all of her struggles, he quickly decided that no one would interfere with his decision to marry the lady of his dreams. Parthenia reminded him so much of his own dark-skinned mother. Not long after they married on October 7, 1916, Parthenia gave birth to their first child, a lovely daughter, Thelma. She looked so much like Charles D., that Parthenia named her Charles Thelma.

Charles D. kept in touch with all of his brothers and sisters despite moving to Louisville. Dudley had moved to New York City while Ellis moved to San Francisco, California. His brother, Detricth died as a young man in Hopkinsville. Solomon married and began his family but always kept in touch with Charles D.

Charles D., his sisters, and brothers were looked down on by their father's sister, Ellen. She remained in Hopkinsville where she reared two daughters, Cornelia and Bobbie. Cornelia was named after her maternal Grandmother, Ms. Cornelia Wallis. Bobbie and Cornelia became schoolteachers and would travel to Louisville years later to stay in the home of Charles D. and Parthenia when they attended the Colored Education Association meetings. In those days, there were very few overnight accommodations for people of color. Charles D. and Parthenia gladly welcomed them into their home to stay overnight. Charles D. kept in touch with his brothers and sisters who lived in Louisville, and he also corresponded with his brothers from the east coast to the west coast.

Charles D. was determined to treat his wife as if she were a queen. She was a pretty woman of small stature while he stood over six feet tall. Charles D.'s older sister ridiculed Parthenia. She would send sarcastic valentine cards to Parthenia containing derogatory remarks stating she was ugly and would have ugly black children. Charles D. and Parthenia were very loving and caring parents. They were so happy with the birth of Thelma that they decided to have another child. However, in the year of 1918, a terrible influenza virus spread throughout the entire country. Thelma contracted influenza; however, after careful nursing from her mother she quickly recovered. Approximately two years and nine months after Thelma's birth, Charles D. and Parthenia became proud parents of another baby daughter they named Mildred Naomi who was born on Thanksgiving Day, November 27, 1919. The two little girls of Parthenia and Charles D. were dressed as well as any other children in the neighborhood.

Parthenia, a native of Louisville, Kentucky was born in a house at 11th and Zane Streets. She was one of eight children of Charlie and Luvenia Hamilton. Parthenia's mother died when her youngest living sister, Laura, was only eleven years old. Parthenia mentioned that the last sister actually died as an infant. The sister next in age to Laura was Mollie, who was about

14 years old when their father suddenly decided to marry. Their stepmother did not want the girls, so they were forced out of their father's home to seek shelter. They attempted to live at the Y.M.C.A. where they were given cleaning assignments for work. Charles D. and Parthenia kept in touch with Mollie and Laura. They fed the two young sisters along with their own children before they would even eat themselves. Charles D. established a wonderful relationship with all of his sister-in-laws and one brother-in-law. They all shared many struggles of poverty and hunger. Parthenia's oldest sister Emma moved to Noblesville, Indiana, where she and her husband were proud parents of two sons, Charles and James. All of the other sisters and one brother, Henry Hamilton, remained in Louisville. One of Parthenia's younger sisters, Mattie, was born on December 24th, the same month as Parthenia, born December 23, 1896. Mattie became pregnant at the age 13 by an older man. She gave birth to a baby she named Leona, who later suffered from tuberculosis. Eventually, the child died at seven years old. Later, Mattie married a man named Samuel Green. From this marriage, they became proud parents of a baby boy named Samuel Green, Jr. Parthenia and Charles D. visited this couple frequently. Parthenia kept in touch with her sister, Louise as well. Louise was born November 16, 1898. Charles D. and Parthenia attended Louise and Eddie Ballentine's wedding at their home on Zane Street. Parthenia's one and only brother, Henry Hamilton, was sworn-in as a Louisville police officer in 1928. The minister of his church, Rev. Watson, wrote a letter of recommendation in his behalf so he could get hired. However, Henry enjoyed shooting a game of dice ever so often. One day after a heated argument during a dice game, Henry was stabbed in one of his thighs. He received a severed artery and bled to death before receiving medical attention. All five of the Hamilton sisters who made Louisville their home kept in touch with their oldest sister, Emma, and they all continued to grow an even closer bond with Charles D.

Chapter 3

Charles D. not only worked one job, he constantly maintained two jobs so that Parthenia had the opportunity to be at home to care and nurture their loving daughters. Thelma needed much coaxing to begin to walk. For some reason, she felt safe walking with the aid of a broomstick, whereas Mildred began to crawl, walk, and run. Soon, Thelma not only began walking without the aid of the broomstick but also began running alongside her younger sister.

Charles D. and Parthenia truly believed in God. They became members of the Antioch Baptist Church and both were baptized. They carried their daughters to Sunday school and church even as toddlers. Charles D. and Parthenia were conscientious parents when it came to the complete care of their daughters. Thelma and Mildred received their medical attention from W.H. Witherspoon. Mildred was diagnosed as having a severe visual problem at age three. Charles D. worked many overtime hours to purchase corrective eyeglasses. Through careful observation and notation, the couple felt their children were intellectually inclined. Charles D. and Parthenia began paying Mrs. Sarah Thomas for private piano lessons in their home for both Thelma and Mildred. Mrs. Thomas would walk from 15th and Broadway to 1611 W. St. Catherine to teach lessons to the girls. Mildred would place a clock on the piano to make sure that she practiced only a given time. Both girls were definitely musically inclined but Thelma began to play the piano as though she wanted to do this for the rest of her life. Thelma joined Antioch Baptist Church and was baptized in 1928 at the age eleven. A few years later, Mildred joined the church and was baptized into Antioch. Thelma was asked to assist playing the piano at church. She played at teas and for various religious functions throughout the city as a teenager. Thelma played in joint revivals along with other churches, for example, Antioch, Centennial, and St. Stephen Baptist Church. Two of these churches are still located in the California Neighborhood. Antioch Baptist Church is now located in a newly built church on Dixie Highway in the Shively area of the city. All of these churches continue to provide worshipful services throughout the community. They all have members with long-standing memberships. Some have been members for over 80 years.

Growing up in the California Neighborhood and living on St. Catherine Street meant that Thelma and Mildred would attend the neighborhood schools beginning with Phillis Wheatley Elementary where even Parthenia attended through the eighth grade. Thelma and Mildred made many friends in church and at school, but due to Charles D.'s rigid view of how children were to be raised, he kept them from socializing when not in school. They also could not sit with friends their ages during church services except in Sunday school. Charles D. ruled his house with an iron hand. Parthenia loved him so much that she abided by all of the rules he set for the entire family. He felt it was necessary to not only love, but to protect his entire family. After all, Charles D. was like a knight in shining armor who had swept Parthenia off her feet and disallowed any of his brothers and sisters to interfere with his decision to marry her. Occasionally, Charles D. would allow Thelma and Mildred to play with the nannie's children, Junie Ray and the Calvin children. Thelma and Mildred continued with their piano lessons from Mrs. Thomas. Thelma also continued to focus on playing for churches and citywide functions.

Charles D. began working for the U.S. Post Office in 1927. He also worked for a florist by the name of Schulz. He worked as a chauffeur for

Mr. Schulz and quickly viewed designing flowers as a possible business for himself. Charles D. and Parthenia felt that they needed to focus on both of their daughter's education. When Thelma and Mildred needed new shoes, Parthenia and the girls would walk from 16th & St. Catherine to Preston and Jefferson Streets to the shoe stores. Thelma wore a very large shoe size just like Charles D. Parthenia consistently had a difficult time finding a child-like shoe to fit her long feet. On the other hand, Mildred had tiny feet just like Parthenia. There were never any problems finding just the right fit for Mildred. Charles D. and Parthenia watched their spending closely. Even though Charles D. worked two jobs, providing new shoes for his daughters and wife, he would rebuild his own shoes. He believed in sacrificing for his family. After losing his mother at such an early age and needing to find ways to feed his hungry stomach even as a young child, he was determined to provide all the necessities for his wife and daughters.

Chapter 4

After Charles D. and Parthenia's daughters completed their elementary education, they enrolled into Madison Junior High School located at 18th & Madison Streets. While attending Madison Junior High School, Thelma began to experience her menstrual cycle. While at church one day when Thelma stood up, Mildred pointed to her chair which was blood-stained. Thelma ran into the bathroom. Mildred explained to her that it was only her monthly period and that it was time for her to start at her age. Mildred reassured Thelma that she was okay and that this was just a natural part of life. Parthenia tried very hard to abide by Charles D.'s rules and agreed not to explain or talk about how the body would begin to mature. That left Thelma in the dark not understanding about bodily changes, but Mildred took a keen interest in health and listened to the older girlfriends who had explained to her about menstrual periods and even about the facts of life.

During these years, Charles D. had begun to build up his own successful florist business and fortunately became the first colored florist not only in the city of Louisville but also in the entire state of Kentucky. For a colored man to successfully start his own business and work a full-time job such as Charles D. was quite an accomplishment in the early 1920's in Louisville.

Because Charles D. and Parthenia understood what it was like growing up poor and needing to count every penny, they allowed their customers to charge their purchases. The customers would pay installments until their bills were paid in full. Many colored churches began to order flowers and designs for decorations as well as for their deceased members. Charles D. taught Parthenia to make corsages. This began to be a specialty for her, as this particular type of design fitted her small stature to a tee. Charles D. began to provide wedding decorations and bridal bouquets for many weddings at many local churches. Even though he began to make a profit, it would take Charles D. a few years to make up his mind to begin advertising. Finally, he asked Mr. Cassius M. Clay, Sr. to paint his first sign to put in front of his house so people would be able to walk or drive by and know about his florist business. Little did anyone who lived on St. Catherine Street know that Mr. Clay's son would turn out to be the heavyweight champion of the world. Charles D. and Parthenia allowed Thelma and Mildred to have small pets. Thelma had a rabbit that she named Bunny. Parthenia would get impatient with Bunny at times because Bunny would seemingly lie in her path while she was sweeping. One day Parthenia decided to sweep Bunny out of her way. That was the day Bunny decided to retaliate and jumped on Parthenia. Needless to say, when Charles D. was told of Bunny's boldness, Bunny was quickly orphaned. Also, Mildred and Thelma had a dog they named Pup. One of their very few playmates, David Goodloe, would come to visit them quite often while eating a bean sandwich. Of course, Pup would beg David for a share, and he began to allow Pup to take a bite out of his bean sandwich. At times, he would tell Pup, "You don't have to take a hog bite, Pup!" This, of course, would make Mildred and Thelma giggle for hours.

 Charles D. and Parthenia had many friends at Antioch Baptist Church where they attended with their daughters. However, due to a strong disagreement with the minister, Charles D. decided he and his family would move their memberships. Their family joined the Mount Lebanon Baptist Church. At the time, the minister was Rev. William H. Ballew, Sr. Thelma and Mildred quickly developed close ties to the minister's daughter, Anna

Ballew. Parthenia and Charles D. became very active members. Since Charles D. had already been ordained as a deacon at their former church, he joined the deacon board at Mt. Lebanon. Parthenia joined the deaconess board, the pastor's aide society and many other organizations within the church. Thelma and Mildred spent many hours and many days of the week at church with their parents who became active leaders within the church.

As stated before, Charles D. ruled his house with an iron hand and as his daughters began to enroll in high school he set hard and fast rules that they were never to participate in any dances nor could they attend any sports activities after school. Charles D. did teach Thelma to drive as he had taught Parthenia. Not many of her friends knew how to drive at age 16. However, just because he taught her to drive did not mean she could drive his car wherever she may have wanted to go. Thelma drove to help deliver floral designs and to and from the church.

Thelma continued to play the piano at every religious function when she was asked. Sometimes Charles D. would allow her to play at assemblies in school. Mildred had the ability to play the piano too, but began to rebel at the strict rules set by her father. Mildred could not understand why Charles D. feared a young boy or man might try to take advantage of her youthfulness. At times, Mildred bucked his rules. Charles D. would get his very large belt and beat his daughter. Thelma also received a few of those beatings but not nearly as many as Mildred did. Charles D.'s tight reins actually caused Mildred to become rebellious. Both daughters were very attractive, well dressed, well mannered, and intelligent; but they were kep behind the iron fence and gate. These tight reins caused Mildred to feel that she must run away from home to get from under the iron hand of Charles D. Parthenia was very saddened by the terrible action that Mildred used to get away. Parthenia loved Charles D. very much and knew he was an excellent provider so she stood beside him whenever he made all of the family rules. Since there was talk in the neighborhood about Mildred's boldness to run off and stay with a member of Antioch Baptist Church, Charles D. was not only embarrassed, he was extremely angry with Mildred. When she was talked into returning to her home with her parents and sister, Charles D. gave her what she thought was the beating of her life. In fact, Mildred told her children and her niece, Charlene, that she was once beaten by Charles D. while in the nude and on her menstrual period. This was a beating Mildred would never forget nor one she would ever allow Charles D. to forget. Parthenia cried as her younger daughter had to endure this beating but as always, tried to abide by Charles D.'s steadfast rules. When Charles D. and Mildred had another terrible disagreement, she ran off again staying with a lady who belonged to Mount Lebanon Baptist Church. Parthenia begged Mildred to come home and again Charles D. lashed out with his belt attempting to put fear in Mildred's heart.

Chapter 5

Parthenia not only loved her daughters, she continued to keep in touch with all of her sisters. Many days, Parthenia would get her wagon and walk Mildred and Thelma over to her youngest sister Laura's house. She would quickly fill her wagon with her niece Minervia and her nephew Jimmy. This enabled Laura to have the time to work outside her home and help her husband provide the necessities for their family. Laura and Mollie were truly the closer sisters. If Mollie could have had it her way, she would have been the one to baby-sit for Laura's children. Mollie and Laura met two brothers while they were attending night school and Laura and Mollie became Mrs. Elijah Bennett and Mrs. Jesse Bennett, respectively. Mollie never conceived any children, but you would have thought that Laura's children were hers too. When Parthenia could not help with Minervia and Jimmy, Mollie would always be willing to baby-sit and care for her niece and nephew. She loved them as if they were her very own children. Later in years both Mollie and Parthenia helped with the care of Elijah, Jr. after he was born the night of Thelma's high school graduation.

Parthenia became a very active member of the Eastern Stars and joined the Bettie Morton Chapter. She and Charles D. decided that Mildred and Thelma would join the juvenile chapter of Bettie Morton.

Charles D. did not hold his tongue when expressing his dislikes of dancing and social gatherings outside the church. He voiced his opinion to even many of his customers. Word of his dislikes of partying spread to many people who were involved in social functions. When Thelma entered Central Colored High School, it was a known fact that she would not be attending, participating, or playing for any dances. She was allowed to play only for P.T.A. programs and assemblies.

When Thelma was a junior in high school, one of her classmates, Mary Ruth Smith, encouraged her to learn the Gettysburg Address. When the day came to recite it, her friend laughed and told Thelma that she never tried to memorize it. Thelma did and stood in front of her English class reciting it perfectly. The English teacher, Mrs. Carrie Alexander, was so thrilled with Thelma's accomplishments that she presented her with a book of poems. Charles D. and Parthenia were so pleased. With Charles D.'s love of poetry and his ability to write poetry, he cherished that book after Thelma gave it to him until the day he died. Because of his hard fast rules and his boldness to let others know how he felt about social gatherings, Thelma was made to seek out the students who never participated in any of the gatherings as well. This is when Thelma developed a life-long friendship with Effie Durrett. These two were chosen to be the old maids in the school play when Thelma was in her junior year. Also in her junior year, Thelma entered a talent contest sponsored by the **Louisville Defender Newspaper**. Thelma played the piano so well that she won and received a free trip that year to the World's Fair held in Chicago, Illinois. She was accompanied by her mother, Parthenia, and her sister, Mildred.

Thelma was also chosen by Mrs. Crumes, the music teacher, to play for the graduation class, which preceded hers. When Thelma was a senior in high school, her sister Mildred entered Central. The same rules set down by Charles D. applied for Mildred as well—absolutely, no participation in any social gatherings. Of course, Thelma knew as a senior that she would not get to attend her senior prom. But she was allowed to play for her high school commencement program. Due to Charles D.'s outspoken nature, the school's staff members and students who participated in the social gatherings caused many of them to dislike his beliefs and daughters. His daughters never received much recognition for any of their musical abilities. When Thelma was asked to play for her high school graduation ceremony, her name was not allowed on the program for recognition of her playing the piano. Nor was she ever considered to receive any scholarships or awards for her musical contributions. Despite the fact that there was truly discrimination against people of color throughout the state of Kentucky as well as the country, there was also discrimination even within the colored school system. Because it was not in the social circle, there was little support or recognition. Thelma's graduation class had declared their theme to be "The Contribution of the Negro to American Life." Thelma would certainly live her life upholding that theme.

When Mildred began her junior year at Central Colored High School, Thelma had hoped to enter a local university such as the University of Louisville. After all, she had been born and raised in the city of Louisville. However, due to discrimination laws that the University of Louisville and other local and state college practiced, she was not allowed to enroll. Charles D. was determined that his daughter would be able to further her studies at an accredited college. He was so determined to lend his tall shoulders for his daughters to stand on that after careful consideration and discussion with his wife, the decision was made that Thelma would apply and enroll at Indiana University in Bloomington, Indiana. While doing her weekly grocery shopping at a neighborhood store, Parthenia happily told Mrs. Schuckman, the owner's wife, that Thelma had been accepted into Indiana University. Mrs. Schuckman threw Parthenia's package of meat at her and said, "My Jesse applied to get in there and was turned down! I can't see how your daughter was accepted!" Needless to say, Parthenia decided to move her grocery shopping to another neighborhood store. It was looked upon people of color in those days to maybe finish high school and take whatever job you could get, but not in Charles D.'s mind. He remembered the hard time he had growing up so poorly and Parthenia had told him about the difficult times she and her family members had suffered. They only wanted their children to have a chance at furthering their education to become productive citizens.

Charles D. was accompanied by Parthenia to the campus of Indiana University, but after examining the dorms and housing, Charles D. felt that none was suitable for his daughter, Thelma. He had asked around the colored community for appropriate housing and was introduced to a man by the name of Mr. Lee Johnson who had a sweet wife by the name of Mrs. Addie Johnson. They had allowed their granddaughter, Margaret Johnson, to room and board there and accepted Thelma as well. Charles D. had a long and stern talk with Mr. and Mrs. Johnson and insisted that Thelma return from classes immediately and begin studying around the dining room table as well as after supper. Charles D. had warned Thelma not to indulge in any social dancing and he asked Mr. and Mrs. Johnson to discourage her from accepting any invitations. Thelma had always tried to be obedient to her parents. So hard and fast rules even after she enrolled in college did not upset her nor did they come to her as a surprise. Thelma adjusted well and studied most evenings with Margaret Johnson. Thelma often attended the colored churches in Bloomington on Sundays, alternating between the Methodist church and the Baptist church. Thelma began to play the piano at Rev. Porter's church, which was a Baptist church. Sometimes she would also play at a Methodist Church. Charles D. accepted her playing for a church other than a Baptist church.

Thelma would begin a lifelong friendship with Margaret Johnson but within the next two years, the younger sister of Margaret, Mary Johnson would become an even closer, lifelong and dear friend.

Chapter 6

While Thelma was beginning her freshman year at Indiana University, Mildred had begun her junior year at Central Colored High School. Mildred studied hard, making excellent grades. In the evenings, she would help with the flower business and help Parthenia with the household chores. Mildred missed being with her sister Thelma and soon she too would graduate from Central Colored High School. Charles D. told Mildred that he wanted her to become a doctor. Mildred tried to conform to his very strict and bullish ways and agreed to join Thelma at Indiana University where she was also accepted.

Charles D. knew that if Mildred had the nerve to run off from home twice, he felt that he could definitely not trust her to even be left with Mr. and Mrs. Lee Johnson. So, Charles D. made the decision that Parthenia would move to Bloomington, Indiana and live with both of their daughters so that Mildred could be watched. He also felt that from an economic standpoint, the family would be provided for in a sufficient manner. Charles D. moved their piano from 1611 W. St. Catherine to the home of Mr. and Mrs. Lee Johnson. However, Mildred, Thelma, and Parthenia lived in a house with another family named the Hawes. Thelma was allowed to go to the Johnson's home to practice her piano lessons. However, Mildred was not allowed to go to the library after classes to study. This made it very difficult for Mildred to pass her classes. Therefore, she was not able to make the grades. After her first semester, she and Parthenia left Bloomington. Thelma stayed and continued her classes working towards her Bachelor's degree in Public School Music.

Upon returning to Louisville, Mildred began to take practical nursing classes while working at the old Waverly Hills Sanitarium. Parthenia never gave up on her daughter's hopes and dreams to be a nurse. Mildred would make excellent grades while attending Practical Nursing School. She would work all day aiding and nursing patients and at least three days a week she would spend many hours in class. Then Mildred would come home and help Charles D. with the delivery of his flowers. Mildred would always help Parthenia in the kitchen as well as help her to wash the dishes and complete other household chores. Even though Mildred had graduated from high school, completed her Practice Nursing program, and was working outside their home, Charles D. stood by his strict rules that she was not to attend any social dances nor could she date anyone. When Mildred returned home from work, Charles D. expected her to stay at home and behind the iron fence and gate. Charles D. continued to fear that some man would take advantage of his daughters. He had to take a lot of kidding from some of his fellow co-workers at the post office. Many times Charles D. was told by some of his co-workers that he must be keeping his daughters for himself. Charles D. endured these snide remarks. He always thought about the way his father had mistreated his mother, Hattie, and how John Whitlock chased many women before he remarried. He only wanted to make sure his daughters were not taken advantage of. Mildred wanted to abide by Charles D.'s rules but it was extremely difficult going to church and talking with other young adults when they talked of their dates. Dating was a normal part of life for most young adults, but not for Charles D.'s daughters. Thelma and Mildred would write to each other to share their feelings of being kept away from any young men. Finally, Mildred began to slip out and date. This information leaked back to her father. He confronted her about her dates. This is when she told her father that she decided she must as a young adult woman make her own choices in life that would make her happier. She was very close to Parthenia who of course continued to abide by Charles D.'s strict rules. Mildred informed her mother that she had applied for a government grant that would help her to get into a school to be a registered nurse. However, Mildred would have to move to St. Louis, Missouri to enter training. Needless to say, Charles D. was not thrilled with the idea of Mildred leaving town. He still worried that someone would misuse her. But as a mature adult who had a profound love for nursing others, she knew that this was an opportunity to serve others, break from up under Charles D.'s strong upper hand, and become the nurse she knew she could be. Even though this decision saddened Parthenia, Mildred assured her mother that she would be fine.

Chapter 7

As Mildred was preparing to leave for St. Louis, Missouri, Thelma was completing all of her required classes for her to be awarded her college degree. In the meantime, while Thelma was in her senior year, she met a young man by the name of Leon Henderson Hampton. Leon was a native of Bloomington, Indiana. He worked meager jobs and had been reared only by his mother, Loras Ellen Gray. Leon attended the Methodist church in Bloomington and at times Thelma would attend with him. Leon would work more than one job and often time missed seeing Thelma. Sometimes Leon would work a job shining shoes. Leon had learned the art of whistling. Many days Leon would walk by the boarding home of the Hawes' and whistle a beautiful, romantic tune. Thelma would hear him and her ears would perk. She had not dated any other man and being an adult, she would simply walk out on the porch to greet Leon. Some days Leon and Thelma would go to the tennis courts on the campus of Indiana University and play a game or two of tennis. Thelma had taken tennis as an elective and delighted at the chance to beat Leon at this particular sport. Thelma paid only fifty-cents for her tennis racquet.

Thelma and Leon began to date but this did not delight Charles D. Mr. and Mrs. Hawes had informed Charles D. and Parthenia that Thelma had dated Leon Hampton and noted that she had been spending a lot of time with him. Charles D. was very disappointed and informed Thelma that he did not approve of their friendship. Charles D. had begun to ask several people in the community about Leon's background. When he learned that Leon had come from a single parent home, he was even more disappointed. Leon and his sister, Gladora, had been reared by a very religious and hard working woman who worked in service ironing clothes for wealthy people. She even cooked for them. It was honest work that Loras was doing but that was unsatisfactory as far as Charles D. was concerned. Never mind that Leon's sister, Gladora, was working and attending classes at Indiana University. Even though she did not graduate, she had many credit hours that she completed. Never mind that Leon and Gladora had been reared with the belief that God would one day make sure they would have fulfilling and happy lives. They were brought up to attend and take active roles in the church. Even as young adults, when they met Charles D.'s daughter, Thelma, they attended church regularly; of course is was not a Baptist church. Charles D. was always very opinionated and actually believed that the Baptist faith was the only faith acceptable for him, his wife, and both daughters.

When it was time for Thelma to graduate from Indiana University, she received her degree of Bachelor of Public School Music on November 24, 1939. Her parents were extremely proud. They both were excited to have a college graduate. Charles D. continued to feel it was necessary that even as an adult college graduate, Thelma must return to Louisville and abide by his rules. Yes, Charles D. paid his daughter's tuition even though she received some help from Mrs. Montana Grinstead, a Caucasian woman who encouraged Thelma to finish school. Charles D. really sacrificed for his daughter's chance to receive higher education, but when Thelma wanted to apply for jobs in the field of music in other cities besides Louisville, Charles D. quickly objected. Thelma had been given the opportunity to apply for a job at RCA but the job was located in another state. Thelma had begun to like Leon Hampton very much. But due to the fact that she loved her parents and the fact that she had always tried to be very obedient, she left Bloomington with her parents and bid farewell to Leon.

When Thelma returned to Louisville, she decided to correspond with Leon. She began to play for churches again. Thelma had learned to play classical music as well as some popular music. Of course, her love for anthems and hymns would never cease. But in Louisville at that time, there were no positions for people of color to play classical music except at their churches for perhaps Christmas or Easter concerts.

Thelma tried to apply for teaching positions within the Old Louisville Public School System but most jobs went to people in the social circle. Even though Thelma had graduated from an accredited university and was certainly qualified to teach, she was not considered for a permanent job as a teacher. Charles D. told many of his co-workers that he was not paying anyone, as some parents may done to do, to get his daughter or son a job as a teacher. Thelma continued to write Leon but also decided to play and accompany a friend who had graduated from Kentucky School for the Blind. Thelma teamed up with Gladys Watts who had one of the most melodious soprano voices in Louisville and even in the state of Kentucky. They played and sang at teas and churches throughout the city and state. One day Thelma was able to talk Gladys into trying out for the Ted Mack Talent Show in New York City. Thelma was making a small amount of money playing for churches and she also helped Charles D. and Parthenia with the delivery of his floral arrangements. When Thelma and Gladys received word that Gladys had been accepted to appear on the Ted Mack Talent Show, Charles D. and Parthenia wished them both well and off to New York City both the young women went. After Thelma and Gladys arrived at the studio, Thelma was sadly informed that she would not be able to accompany her friend Gladys due to the fact that she was not a part of their local musician union. Thelma cheered for Gladys anyway and the two young women enjoyed their trip to New York City. They had so much to tell all their friends at Mt. Lebanon Baptist Church about the city and their rewarding experience.

Chapter 8

After Thelma returned from New York City to Louisville, she began substitute teaching in the old Louisville School System. She continued to write Leon letters regarding their future together. Thelma had been certified by the state of Kentucky and was qualified to become a schoolteacher anywhere in the state. One day, Thelma received a letter from the state school system offering her a job as a band instructor at Benham High School in Benham, Kentucky. She was familiar with this small city because as a youngster she had visited this city with her parents and sister when they attended a state Baptist convention. Immediately she made up her mind that she wanted to teach in Benham. She knew this city was located in a very mountainous terrain but she was eager to use her musical education to pass along to others. After she told Parthenia about her decision to move to Benham, Kentucky to teach, Parthenia gave Thelma five dollars and her bus fare to Benham and wished her daughter the best in embarking upon her very first permanent teaching position. After Thelma arrived in Benham, she was greeted by a familiar face. The principal of the school was the same Mr. Matthews who had also been a delegate to the Baptist convention that she had attended years before with her parents. Thelma felt very comfortable in her surroundings and quickly began to settle in. She could hardly wait to write Leon and let him know of her new address. They corresponded for months before he was able to save enough money and visit her in the mountains of Benham. Thelma's requirements were to teach fifth grade subjects. This small school began its curriculum from the first grade through the twelfth grade. Also, Thelma was able to start the first marching high school band at Benham High School. She was thrilled at the thought of being able to share her talents and teach many students to play various instruments as well as how to read music.

She truly loved music and this was a great opportunity to incorporate into the children's minds that they could play instruments as well as complete their scholastic assignments and apply for scholarships to further their education.

Leon was eager to visit Thelma. He continued to work several jobs in Bloomington, IN, until he had enough money saved to visit to propose to marry her. In fact, Leon wrote Charles D. and Parthenia requesting their daughter's hand in marriage to receive a penny postcard saying that they did not want their daughter marrying a shoeshine boy. Of course, that naturally hurt Leon's feelings, but it did not change their love for each other. After Thelma taught at Benham for two years, she left that mountainous town with the hope she had influenced the children whom she had taught to use their medical talents and keep pursuing their education. Thelma had made up her mind to return to Bloomington, Indiana. On December 27, 1941, with her sister Mildred standing beside her, Thelma exchanged her wedding vows with Leon and they became one.

Charles D. was disappointed about his daughter marrying someone that he didn't approve of, but he also knew that Thelma had been a very obedient daughter who finished college and was willing to work. Thelma had decided it was time she was able to make some adult choices for herself. She and Leon returned to Louisville staying with Charles D. and Parthenia. Charles D. did not object because he was actually happy to have his daughter back at home, even though she had chosen the man that she wanted to be married to for the rest of their lives.

Leon immediately began looking for jobs in Louisville. He had been as independent as possible while living in Bloomington and wanted to provide a place for him and Thelma to live as quickly as possible. There were very few types of jobs available for those without a college degree from an accredited school of higher learning. It seemed as though there were even fewer jobs for people of color to be hired for jobs that paid higher salaries coming or for anyone coming from another city and state.

Since Pearl Harbor had been bombed December 7, 1941, Leon decided that he would join the United States Army to serve his country. By 1943, Thelma and Leon decided they would like to become parents. Thelma joined Leon in Dyersburg, Tennessee, where he was stationed. About ten months later, Thelma visited her doctor and was informed that she was expecting their first child. Leon's mother, Loras, came to visit with them and stayed during the delivery of their first child, a son named Leon Henderson Hampton, Jr. Thelma and Leon were such proud parents. Leon received orders that he was to be shipped out to Okinawa, Japan. Thelma bought a bus ticket to return to Louisville while Loras bought her bus ticket to return to Bloomington, Indiana. It wasn't long after those departures that Leon left Tennessee with orders to report for his assignment in Japan.

When Thelma arrived at the bus station in Louisville with her young son, Charles D. and Parthenia could hardly contain themselves. Leon Jr. was their first grandchild and the fact that they never conceived a son delighted them even more. Charles D. and Parthenia asked Thelma to please stay with them so that they could get to know and love their first grandchild. In fact, Charles D. and Parthenia asked Thelma if they could have Leon Jr. Her reply was 'only if you let me be his nurse'. That answer made them one of the happiest couples in the city of Louisville. Charles D. was still working at the post office while his florist business had begun to grow. However, he always found time to spend with Leon Jr. just to hold and touch him. Thelma began to help Charles D. deliver his floral arrangements as she had in the past. She also decided she should pursue a career of teaching in the old Louisville School System. So once again she applied to be hired as a full-time certified teacher. It was extremely difficult in those days for her to be hired permanently. Thelma decided to accept the position of substitute teaching. She had no problems getting a babysitter. Leon Jr. was the love of Parthenia's life. She was more than happy to care for him even 24 hours a day. Thelma decided to also work for the *American Baptist Newspaper* on the days that she was not called to substitute. Charles D. was a staunch deacon in Mt. Lebanon Baptist Church. The pastor, Rev. William H. Ballew, Sr. was more than delighted to have Thelma work at *American Baptist Newspaper* where he was the manager. Thelma had been such a close friend to his daughter, Anna Elizabeth. Anna Elizabeth had left town and married Henry Medlock, but she and Thelma corresponded with each other and shared news of their first-born children, Leon Jr. and Roberta Medlock.

Thelma saved her money along with the money that Leon Sr. sent to her. By the year 1946, Leon was discharged from the U.S. Army and returned to Louisville, KY. Right away Leon began looking for work. He did not mind catching the city bus and waiting for hours until he could go from business to business filling out applications. Since he had written so much to Thelma and even sent many gasoline rations to her father, Charles D., he had gotten used to writing until his fingers would cramp. But again it seemed as though there were very few good paying jobs for people of color, regardless whether they had served their country. Charles D. decided that he would go to the courthouse and bargain for a small shotgun-style house in his neighborhood that Leon and Thelma could afford to purchase. Charles D. was determined to keep his grandson and daughter, Thelma nearby. Mildred came to visit after completing her nursing program. She became the registered nurse that she knew she could become. She too was thrilled to love and hold Leon Jr. Thelma and Leon agreed to use the money that they had saved and purchased their first home at 1037 South 17th Street. Parthenia was pleased that Thelma was going to live around the corner. She and Charles D. were sincere about their request to keep and rear Thelma and Leon's first child. Leon Sr. did not get to join in on that decision but accepted their yearning to keep his son. After all, he could walk around the corner and get to visit with his first child. Leon was unhappy about this incident but threw himself into a busy search for a steady paying job. He applied at the Veterans Administration and received a job at the Old Nichols Hospital located in the south end of Louisville. Leon and Thelma had no car at this time but Leon gladly caught the city bus to and from home to earn a living for his family. Many nights Leon Sr. stood on the bus stops waiting for transfers to return home after midnight. There were never offers of a ride home from Charles D. even in the winter when it was bitter cold and the temperature was below zero.

After World War II, there was a boom of babies born. Thelma and Leon became parents again. This time they became parents of a sweet girl, Charlene. Yes, Charlene named for Charles D. despite the fact that Leon had hoped to name her Gloria Jean and even had written this particular name he chose in her baby book only to have a line drawn through it and be replaced with Charlene Hampton. Mildred, Thelma's sister came to visit again from St. Louis, Missouri. She was happy for Thelma and Leon. Mildred had been dating a young man in St. Louis and told Thelma about the possibility of marrying this young man. After a short visit, Mildred returned to St. Louis to continue her nursing career.

Chapter 9

Mildred continued nursing at a local hospital, Homer G. Phillips, where she was able to care for many people. She also had begun dating a young man named David Furnace Harris who had moved to the city from San Antonio, Texas. He was a very tall, slender, and handsome gentleman who had enrolled at Stowe's Teacher's College. He left to serve his country joining the U.S. Army just as Leon Sr. had done. They both decided to spend part of adulthood serving their country. They felt their lives would be more meaningful as patriotic citizens to their country despite difficulty finding adequately paying jobs. Mildred placed the announcement of her marriage to David placed in the local newspaper in St. Louis. Of course, she informed her parents of her engagement and upcoming marriage to David. After Charles D. learned that David was brought up in the Methodist church, he refused to attend their wedding. However, Parthenia's sister, Mattie, took a bus to St. Louis and stood beside her niece. Charles D. continued to be bullish in his ways to attempt to control the lives of his daughters. Surely, he must have realized that an adult child who had pursued a nursing degree and secured a decent paying job had the right to decide about choosing the person she had fallen in love with and decided to marry to become one. This, of course, was the decent thing to do according to the standards that he had preached to his family for years. Charles D. being the staunch deacon that he was even visited couples living together as man and wife without ever actually marrying. Charles D. called this 'waiting' on people who he felt were living in sin. His own two daughter had decided not to live like that, but he stubbornly refused to be a part of their weddings. As a florist and having the ability to design some of the most beautiful floral arrangements ever made, he could have easily designed each of his daughter's wedding bouquets and added a very special personal touch. However, Mildred's marriage went on without the presence of her parents. Mildred and David were so in love that they did not wait a year before they became parents to a lovely baby girl whom Mildred named Parthenia after her own mother. Baby Parthenia was born in the same month as her parents, but on November 12, 1948. Thelma was elated about the fact that Mildred was about to become a mother and took a bus headed to St. Louis to be present when baby Parthenia was born. Of course, Thelma was not worried about who would keep Leon Jr. and Charlene. Parthenia had become the number one babysitter when Thelma was substitute teaching and while Leon was working at the Old Nichols Hospital. That gave Thelma the opportunity to be by her sister's side and assist Mildred after she was discharged from the hospital where Mildred was employed as a nurse.

Mildred was so excited about being a mother. She made several trips to Louisville to allow Parthenia and Charles D. to love and kiss on their grandchild. She and David were so in love that the next year on December 11, 1949, they were proud parents of another darling baby girl. She looked a lot like her daddy and was named Davida Naomi Harris. As Mildred's middle name was Naomi and Davida was able to have both of her parent's names. Mildred began to work part-time and also met one of her cousins who was a student at Homer G. Phillips Hospital. Mildred was able to get her cousin Gene Williams to occasionally babysit for her. She was thrilled to have her kinfolk help her to watch the children so she could help earn a living and not make it so hard on David to be the only supporter of the family. Mildred also had a lady to come into her home and care for Parthenia and Davida so she could continue her nursing career. After David was discharged from the U.S. Army, he began to work and attend college. Mildred also began to attend the Methodist church on a regular basis with her husband David, and like her father, she wanted their family to be raised in the church. This move angered Charles D., but he could not control his adult, married daughter's choice of what type of church to attend. Mildred and David would continue to visit her parents in Louisville and especially at the holidays. These visits made Parthenia especially happy. She was always delighted to have Little Parthenia and Davida come to visit. Thelma's children also were very happy to play with their younger cousins whom they had grown to love so much. As Mildred and David began to work and save their earnings, Charles D. was eager to assist them in purchasing their first home. In fact, it was Thelma, Charles D., and Parthenia who helped to put the down payment on Mildred and David's first home. Thelma had thought about how Charles D. had gone to the courthouse and bargained for she and Leon's house at an auction and she wanted to see her sister happy in her own home.

Chapter 10

Thelma and Leon continued to work hard and care for their children. Leon was truly thankful to get a home of his own. He painted and cleaned their home so well that many neighbors remarked that his property had never looked so nice. Leon may have been very poor growing up and was reared by a single mother, but that didn't keep him from having a lot of pride when he was able to become a homeowner. Thelma knew Leon had talked about wishing he could have the opportunity to enroll and attend college. Even though it had been over a decade since Thelma was denied admittance to the University of Louisville, the doors were still shut to people of color. Leon decided to attempt to work and attend Municipal College. He carried his baby girl on a pillow. Many people could not understand why Leon would carry Charlene around on a pillow as though she were a lump of gold. The members only laughed when they saw him coming and carrying her as he walked into the church. Leon decided to get baptized by Rev. William H. Ballew and become a member in good standing. All of the members at Mt. Lebanon knew Parthenia and Charles D. kept Leon Jr. in their home. They were told about the time this couple would take driving Thelma and Leon Jr. around the city to find Pet Milk, which was the only milk Leon Jr. could drink as an infant. Also, the members marveled at the outfits Parthenia would purchase for Leon Jr. Many stated he was a showcase every Sunday morning. They could not understand Leon Sr.'s love for his baby girl. After all, he did not get to make the choice that Leon Jr. would be reared by his maternal grandparents, Charles D. and Parthenia. Leon gave Thelma the option of continuing to play the organ and piano at church while he attended to their baby girl.

As Leon and Thelma continued to work and rear Charlene and visit Leon Jr. at the Whitlock's home, their yearning to increase their education began to grow. Leon continued to work the second shift at Old Nichols Hospital and in the daytime attended classes at Municipal College located at 7th & Kentucky Streets. It was housed in the old Simmons University buildings. He would proudly take Charlene along showing off how carefully he had braided her hair. Leon loved the idea of caring for his daughter, which freed Thelma to handle the responsibilities of cooking, washing and ironing all their clothes. Leon's mother, Loras Ellen Gray, would visit from time to time and showed Leon different ways to comb Charlene's hair. She also taught him to cook delicious dishes of food. Leon was always in agreement for Thelma to attend all of her choir practices and she also began to give private piano lessons in their home.

Thelma and Leon loved taking their daughter to church even as a toddler. They enrolled her in Mrs. Margaret Douglas' cradle roll at Mount Lebanon. As a toddler, she would attend Sunday school with her friends, Rita Robinson, Joyce Madry, Vincent Barbee, and Edell Powers. One Sunday, while Thelma and Leon were attending church, someone broke into their home. When they arrived home to their dismay, many of Leon's suits, that he had worked so hard to buy, were stolen along with smaller but valuable items. They tried very hard to put all the necessary locks possible in place to keep out intruders.

Leon liked to visit and spend time with his son as often as Charles D. and Parthenia would allow him. Leon and Thelma lived in their home for several years before they were able to purchase their first car. Leon made sure Thelma always had transportation and he would take the city bus to many places to pay their bills as well as to work. One day Leon Sr. was taking

Leon Jr. on a ride on the city bus when one of the Whitlock friends spied Leon Jr. with his father. This woman cried out to Leon Sr., "What are you doing with the Whitlock child?" This touched Leon's heart. He knew that Leon Jr. was his child just as this woman knew also. He could not understand why this woman would insinuate that his very own child did not belong with him at that moment. Leon never forgot that statement and began telling his two children about the nerve of that woman demanding to know why Leon Jr. was with his own father. Leon enjoyed taking his children on the city bus to go to two of the theaters he chose, which were the Lyric and the Grand both located on Walnut Street. In those days, these theaters were for people of color to attend.

Charles D. loved to take Leon Jr. out riding in his car. Many times Charles D. would attempt to feed Leon Jr. healthy food like fruit. One day his grandfather was driving along and asked Leon Jr. whom he called 'Junie' to eat a banana. He tried over and over to coax 'Junie' to eat just one banana. Finally, Leon Jr. turned to Charles D. and said, "Do you want another one to eat?" Charles D. burst out laughing and told all of his family as well as his co-workers at the post office and many of his customers at the florist shop. That was a funny incident that he never forgot in his entire 83 years of life.

Thelma would spend a great deal of her leisure time at Charles D. and Parthenia's home visiting with Leon Jr. Of course, she would always take Charlene along with her. As Leon Sr. would be attending college in the day and working most of the time at the hospital on the second shift. Thelma noticed that Charlene would not talk much as a toddler. Many times she would not even allow Charles D. to hold her. She truly had become a 'Daddy's Girl'. Charles D. and Thelma learned that even though Charlene would not talk very much, she was always listening. When Thelma was about to leave the Whitlock home and Charlene would be sitting on her grandfather's workbench watching him design his flower arrangements, she would quickly attempt to jump down to the floor following her mother. Her mother, as well as her grandparents, got a kick out of her reaction to Thelma's statement about leaving. Then at night when Thelma was about to walk home and it would be dark, Parthenia would always ask Charlene if she was going to walk home or whether she would make her mother carry her. Charlene would always say she was going to walk, but as soon as they approached an open lot that had very large trees and poor lighting, Charlene would quickly raise her arms for Thelma to pick her up and carry her home around the corner.

When Leon Jr. approached the age of five, he was enrolled into kindergarten at the Phillis Wheatley Elementary School where his mother Thelma and grandmother, Parthenia had attended. He became acquainted with his teacher and Charles D. took a very keen interest in Leon Jr. learning to recite poetry. Since Charles D. had such a love for poetry and even composed several poems himself, he was fortunate enough to have some published by the **Louisville Courier-Journal** and **Louisville Times**.

By the time Leon Jr. had been promoted to the third grade, in Ms. Hazel P. Green's class, Charlene was enrolled in Mrs. Bowman's kindergarten class. The fact that the Whitlocks lived across from the school, made it easier for Parthenia and Charles D. to look out after their grandchildren for Leon Sr. and Thelma. They never worried about running late from work.

One day when Charlene was being picked up after her kindergarten class, one of her classmate's mother made a remark as to how sorry she was that Leon Sr. and Thelma's daughter had something wrong with her that kept her from walking. Thelma and Leon Sr. began to laugh and told Mrs. Hall that Charlene could walk fine. She had gotten into a habit of being carried around on a pillow as an infant and toddler; therefore, she liked being carried even at age five.

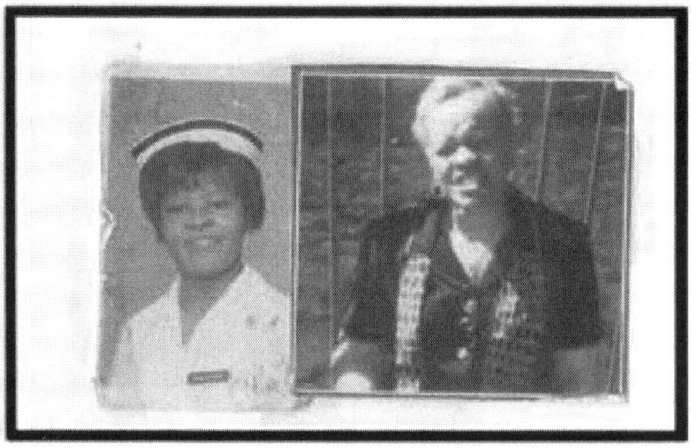

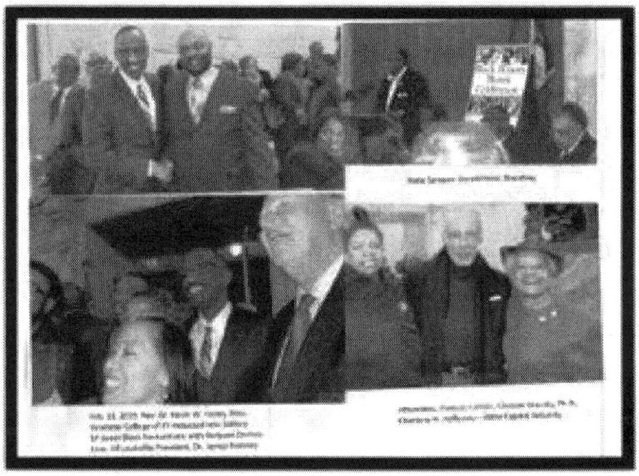

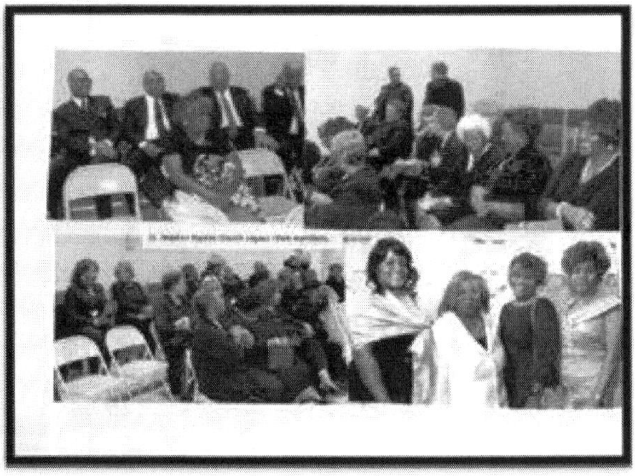

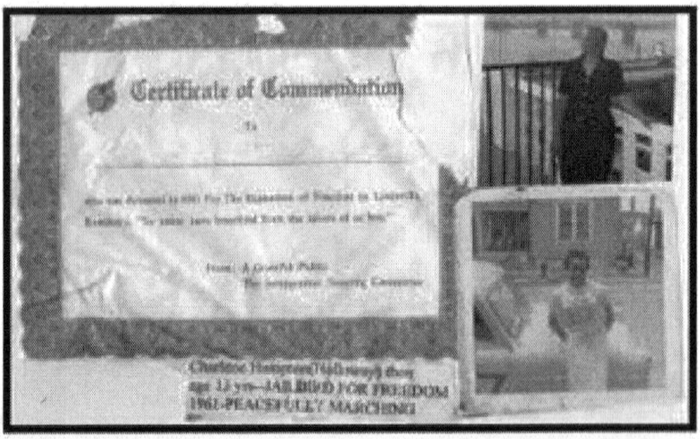
Certificate of Commendation
JAIL BIRD FOR FREEDOM

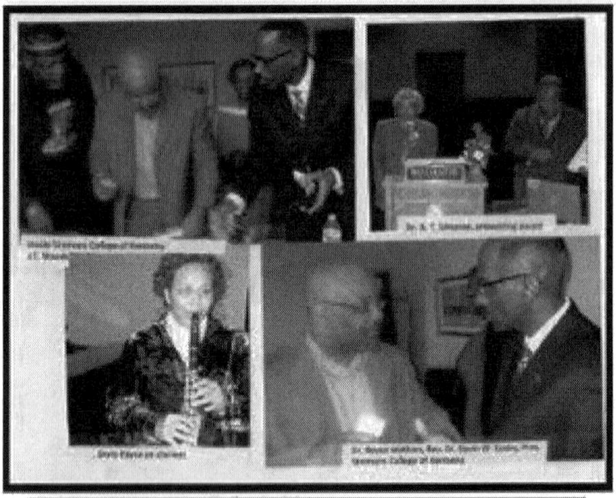

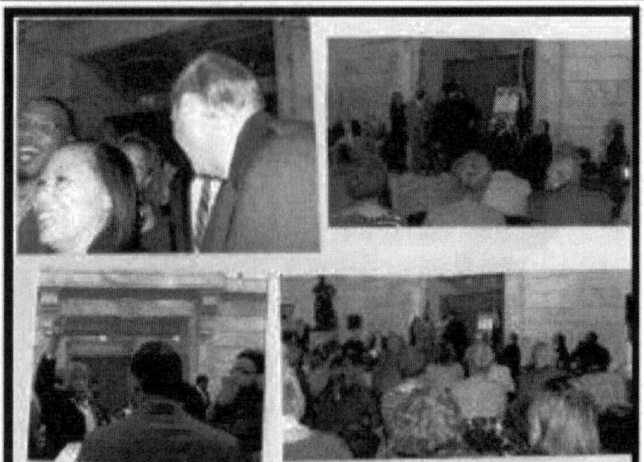

Standing in front of the University of Louisville's Rodin's "The Thinker" statue, Hon. Congressman Romano Mazzoli, Charlene Hampton Holloway and Berta M. Schoposch

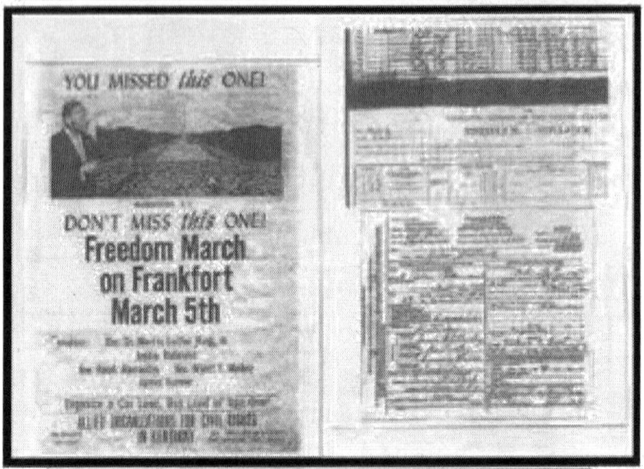
YOU MISSED this ONE!
DON'T MISS this ONE!
Freedom March
on Frankfort
March 5th

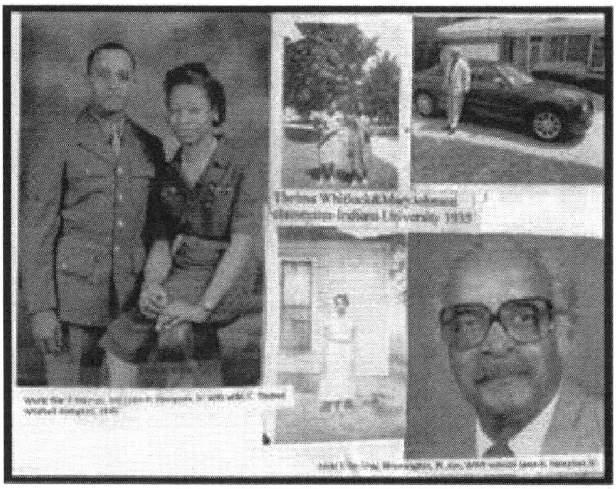
Thelma Whitlock&Mary Johnson

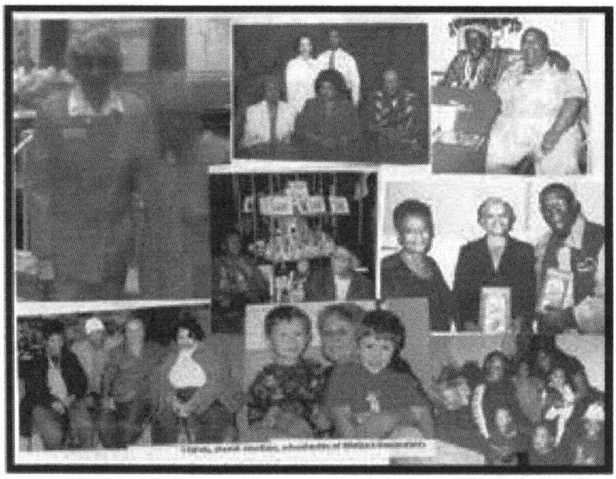

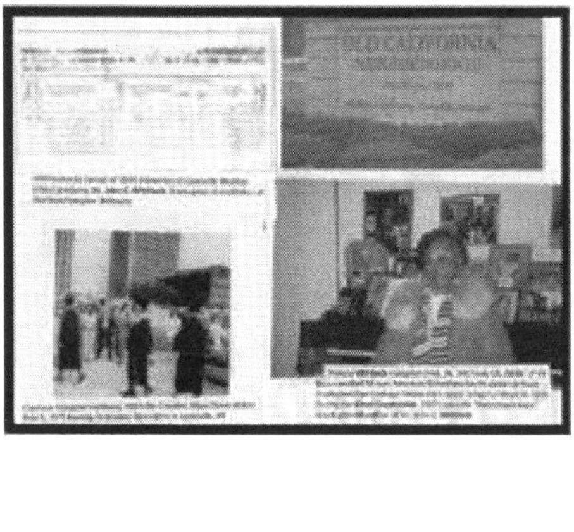

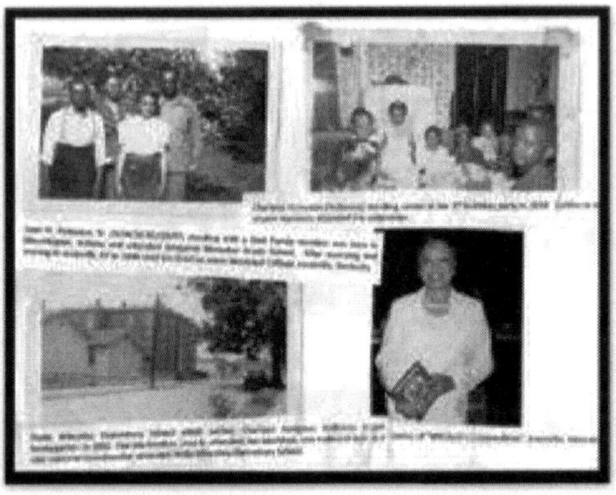

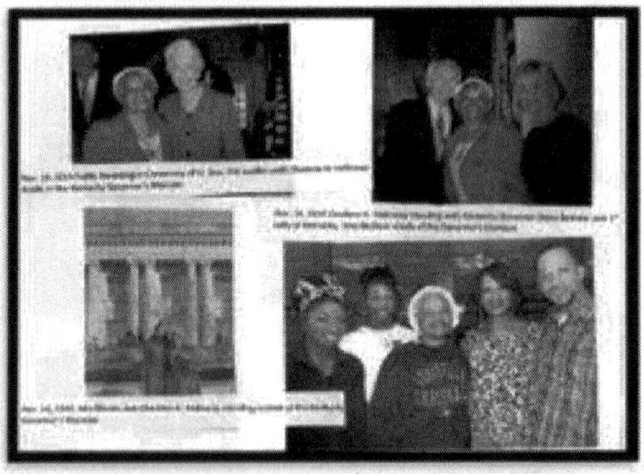

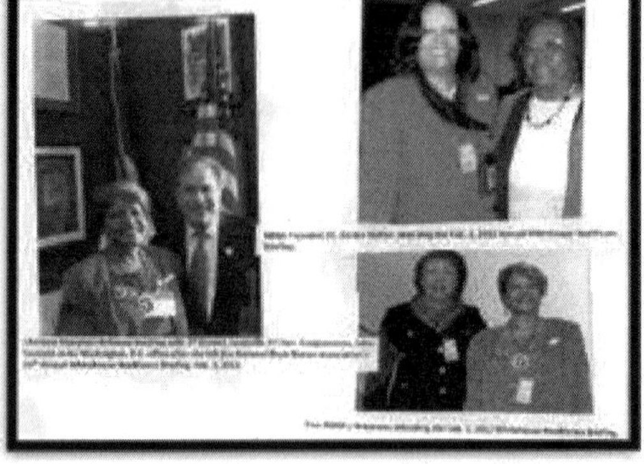

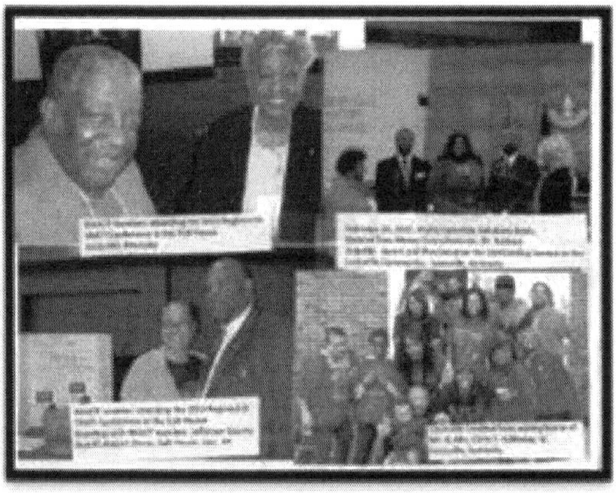

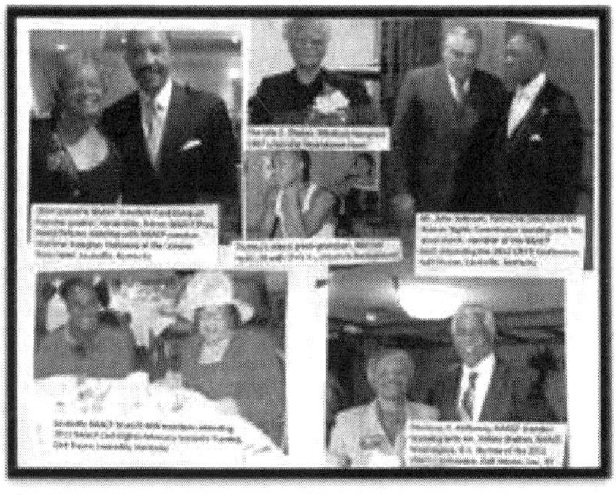

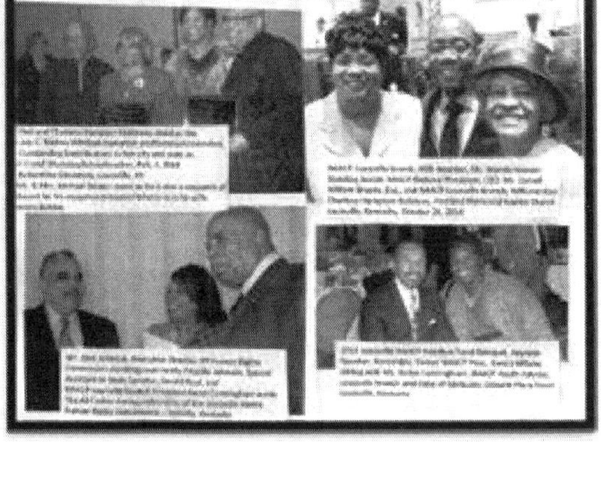

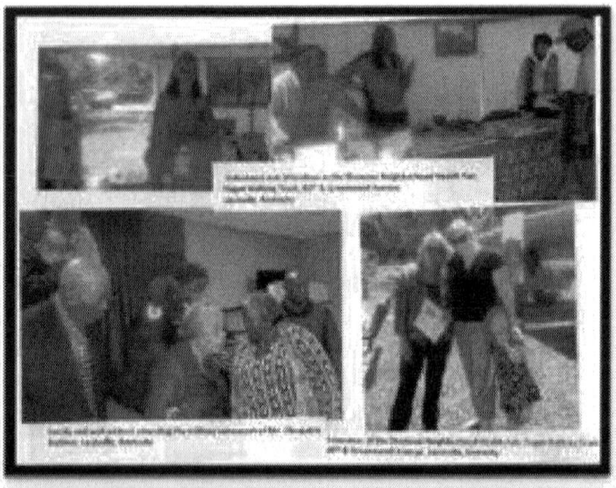

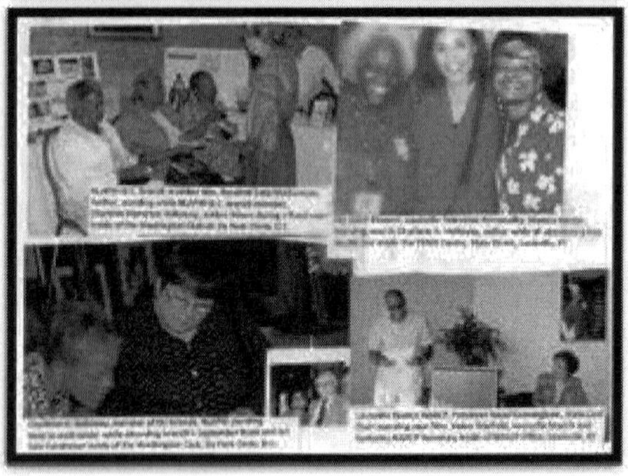

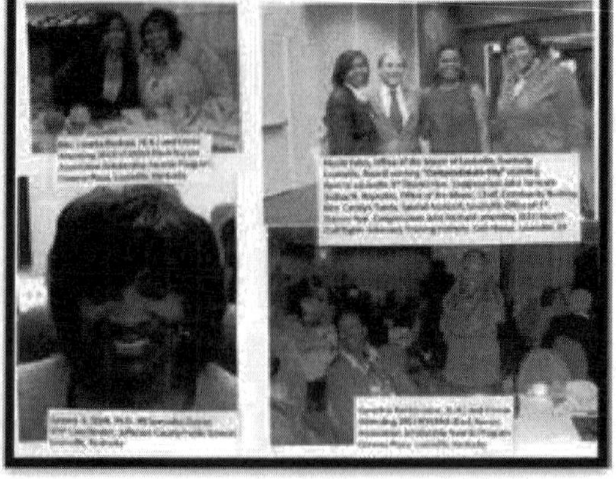

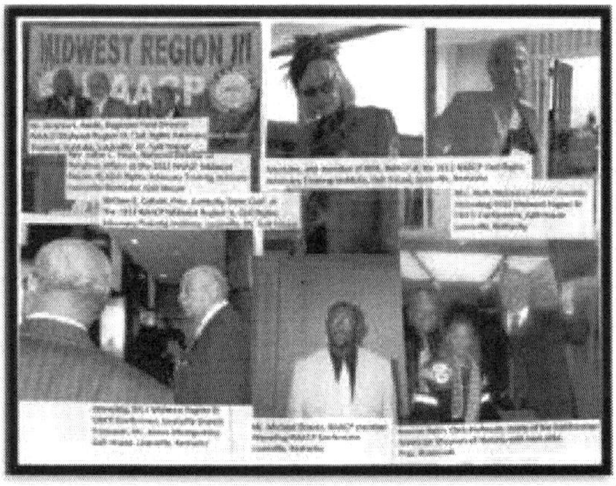
MIDWEST REGION III

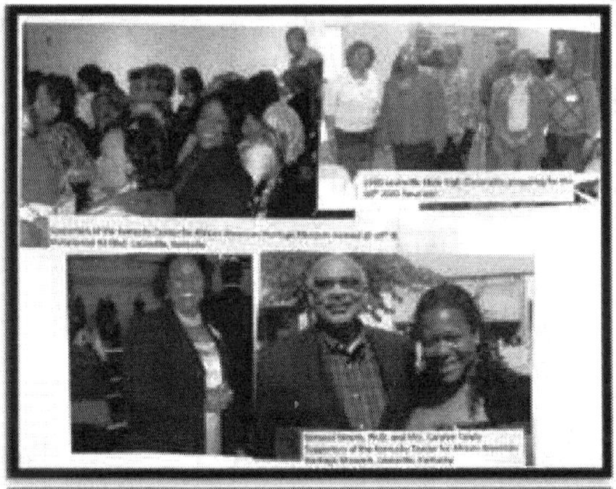

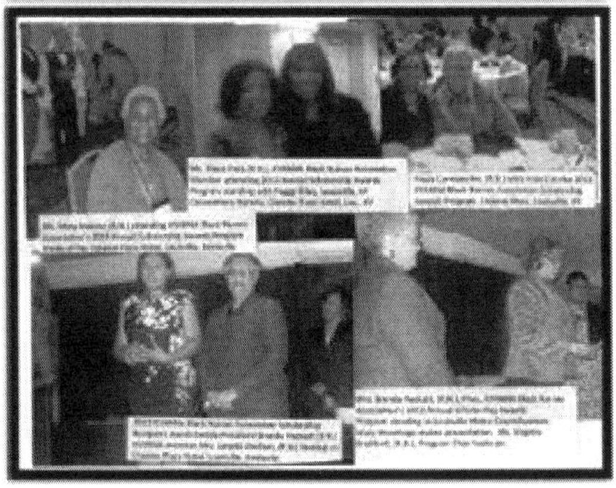

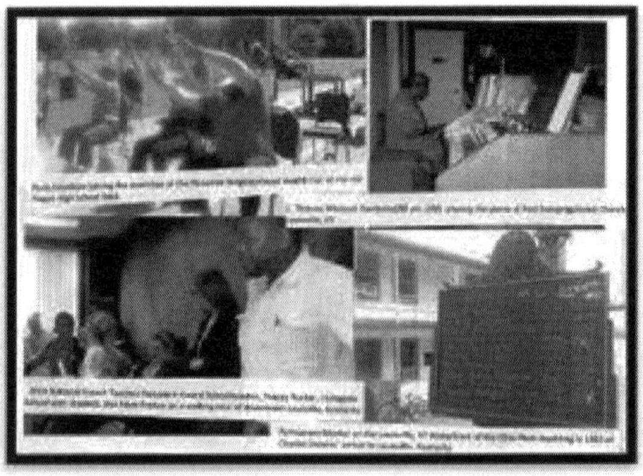

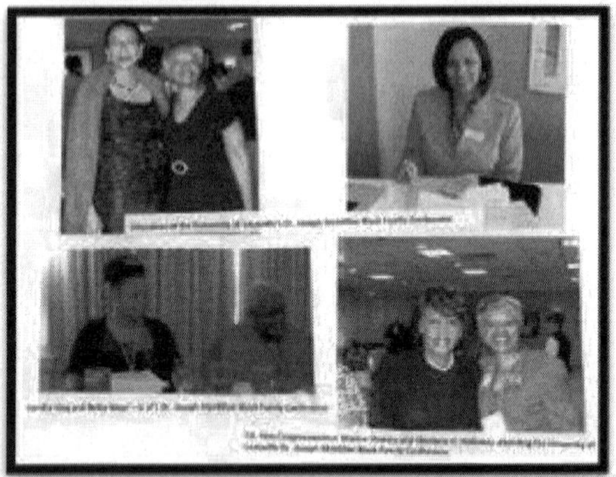

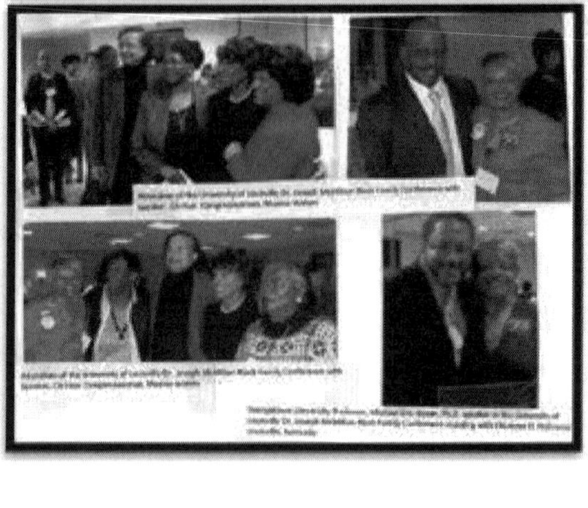

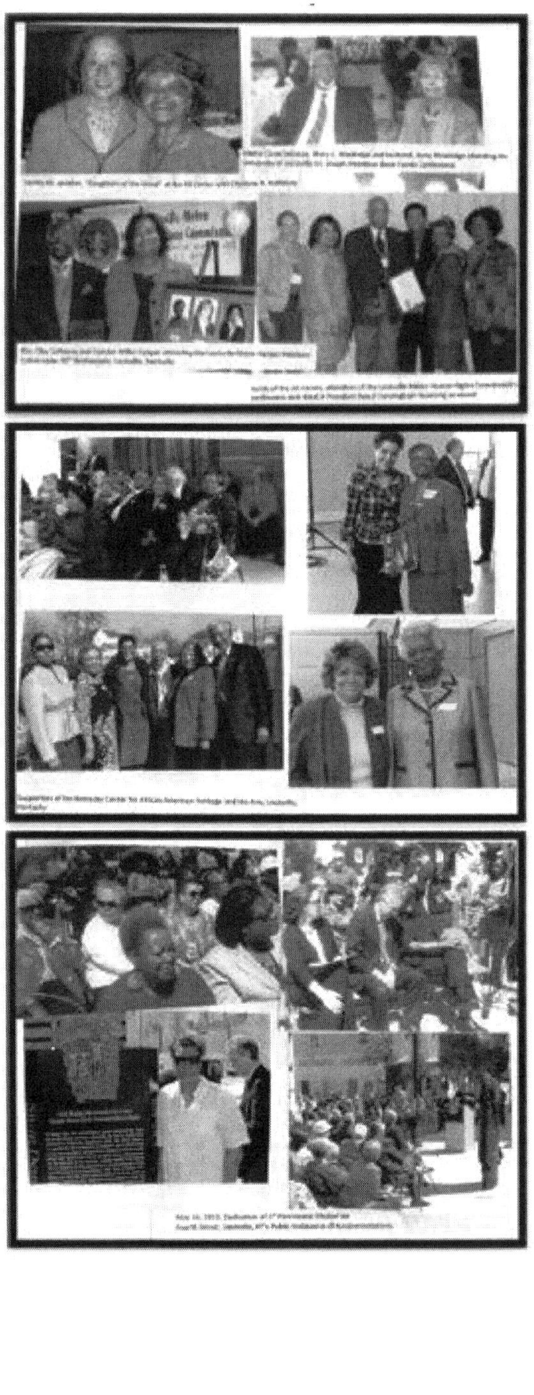

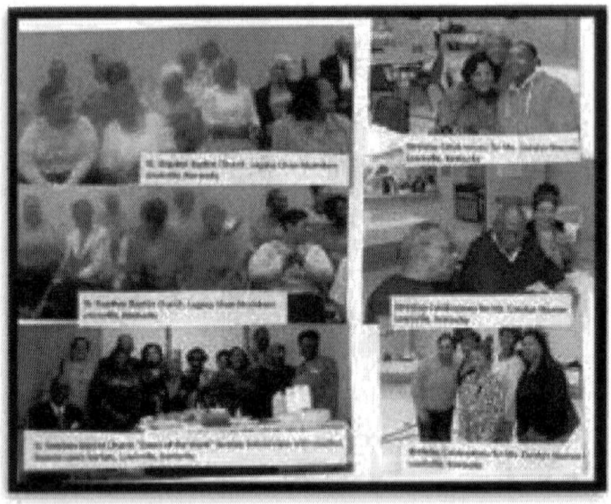

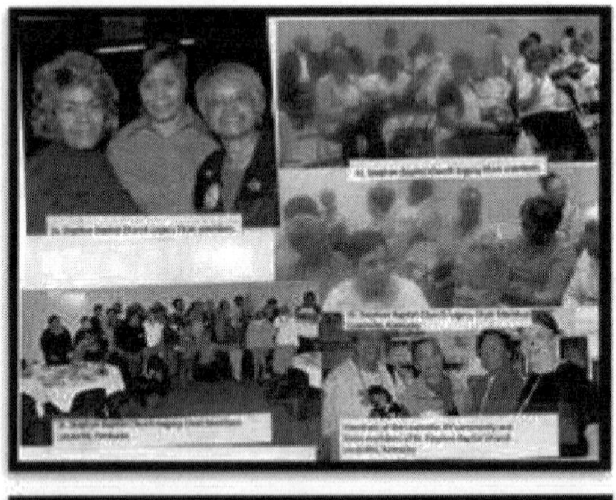

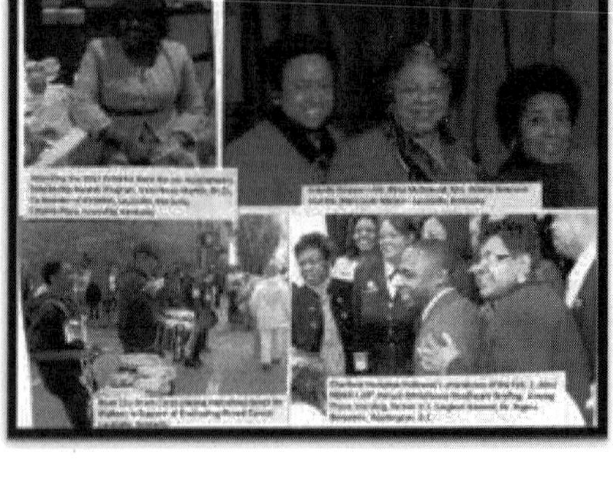

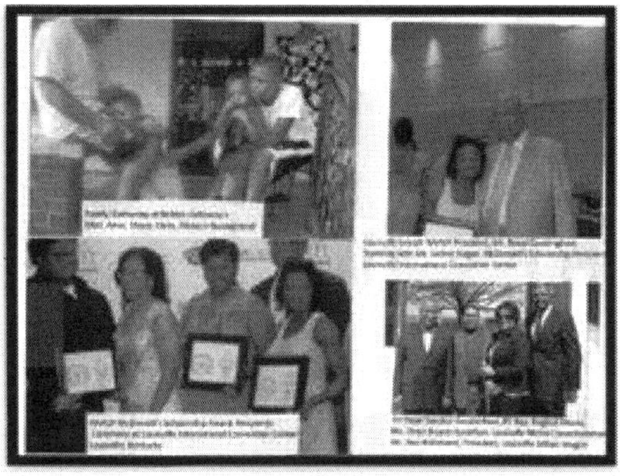

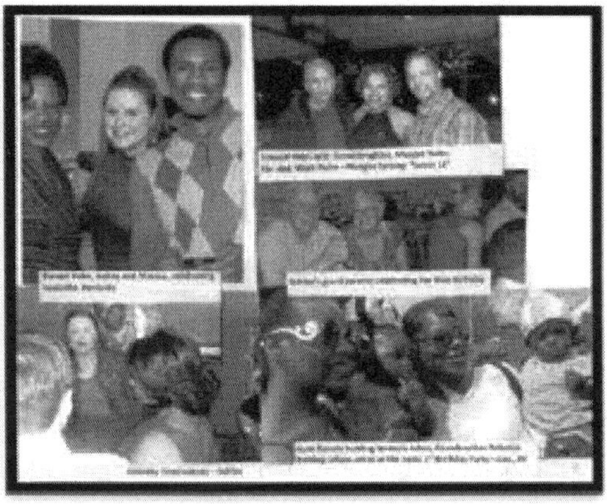

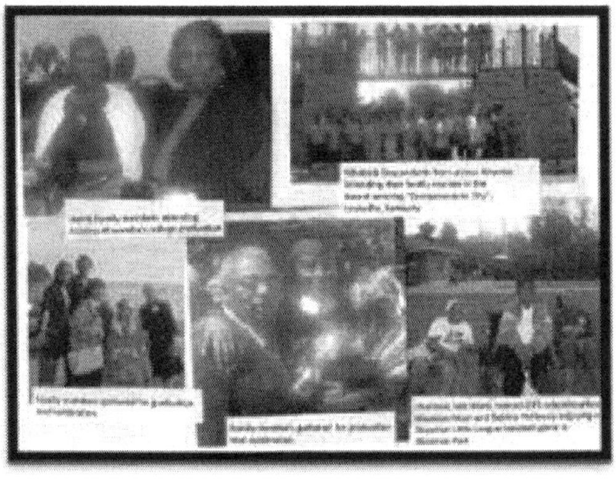

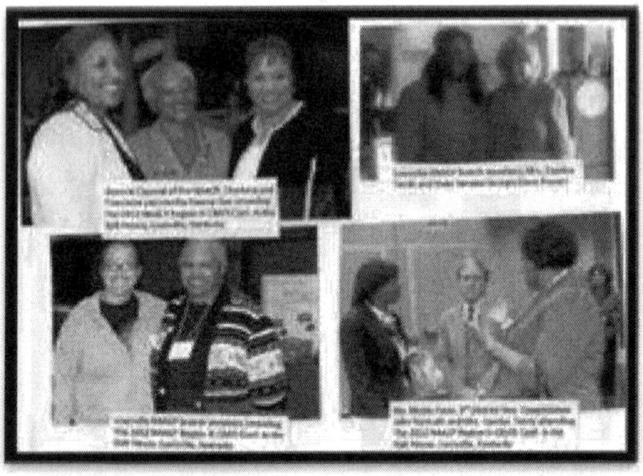

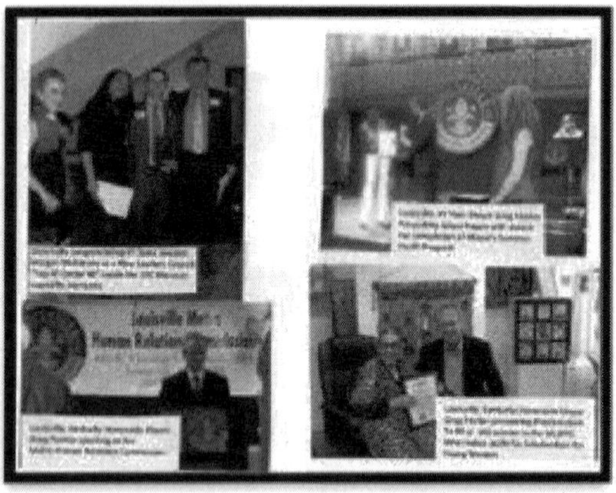

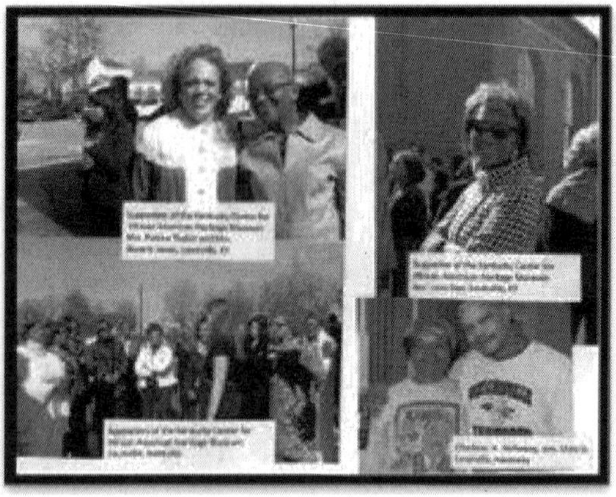

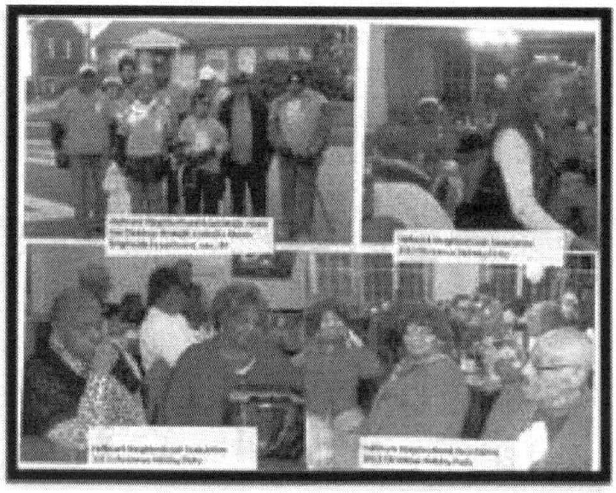

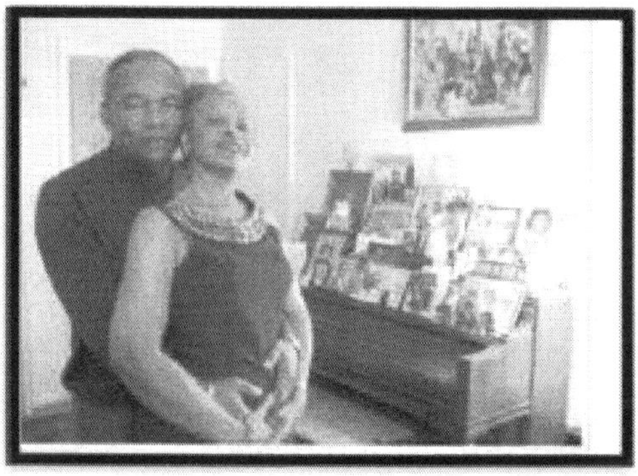

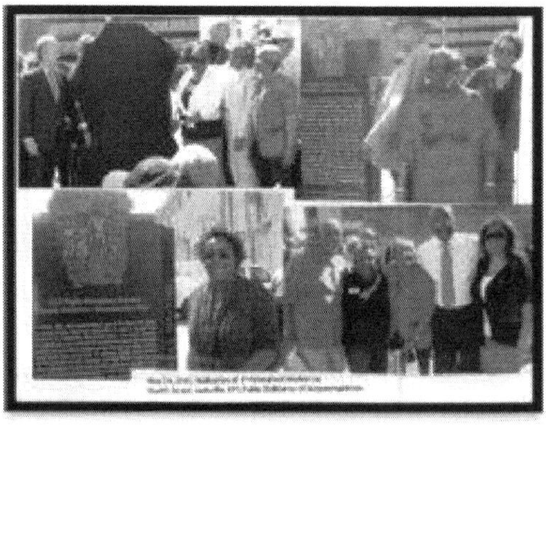

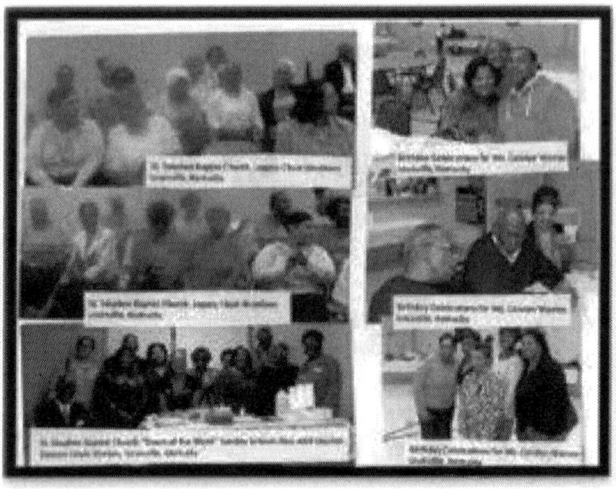

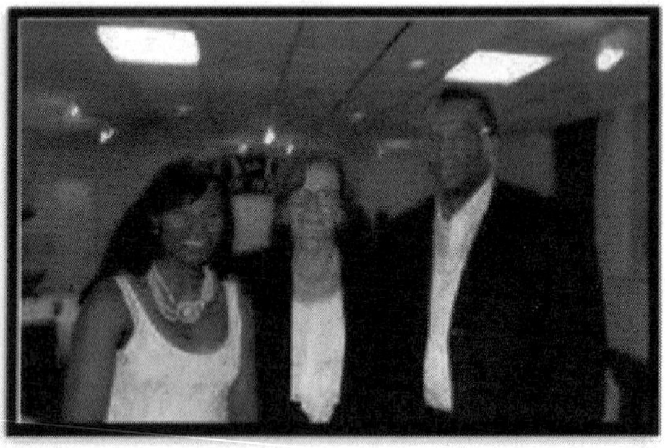

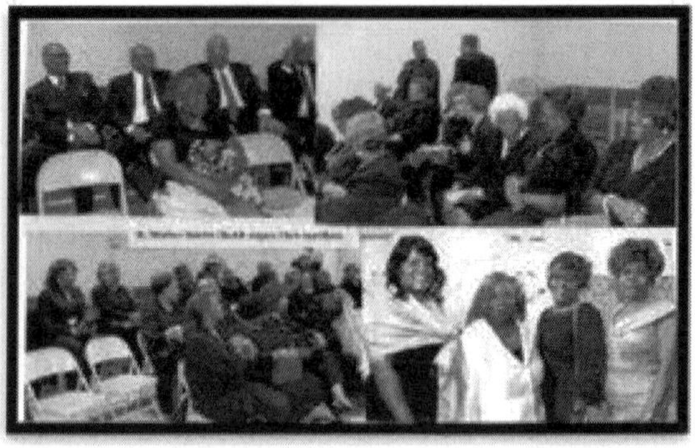

In Loving Memory

Leon Hampton, Jr.

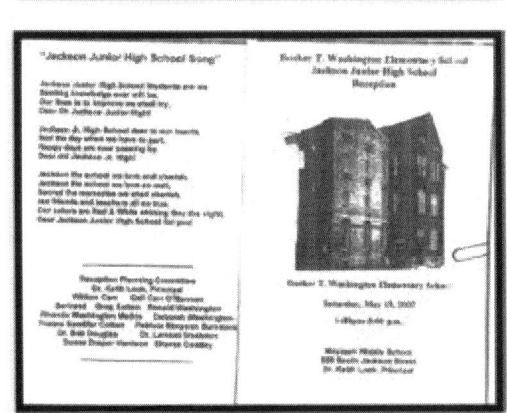

August 28, 1944 to September 10, 2006

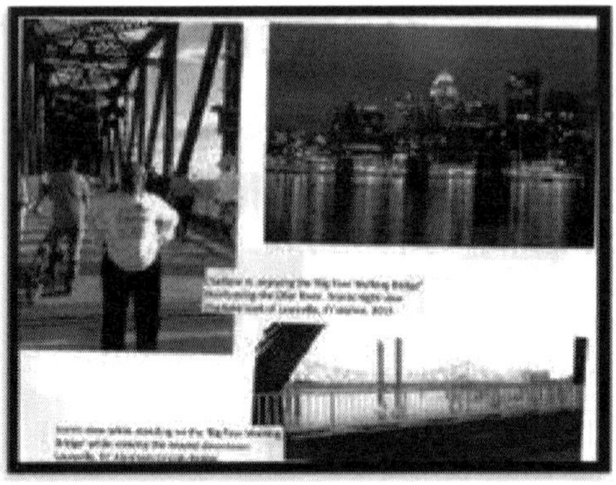

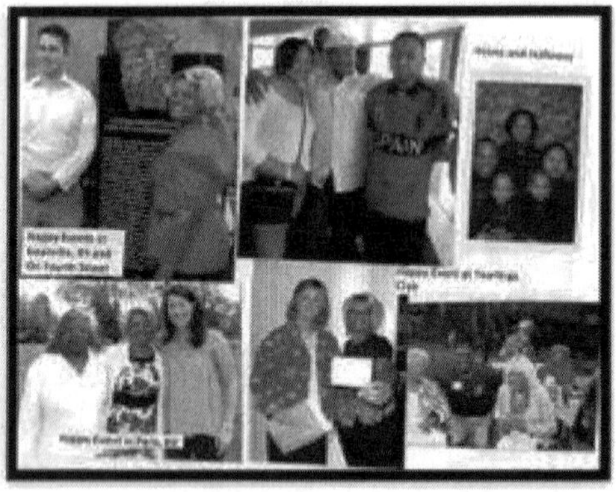

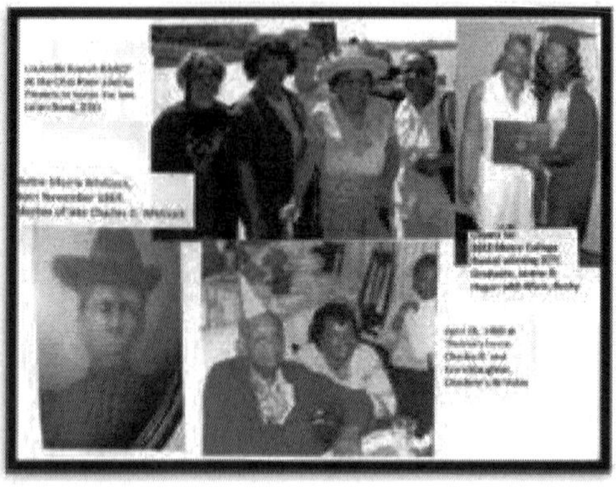

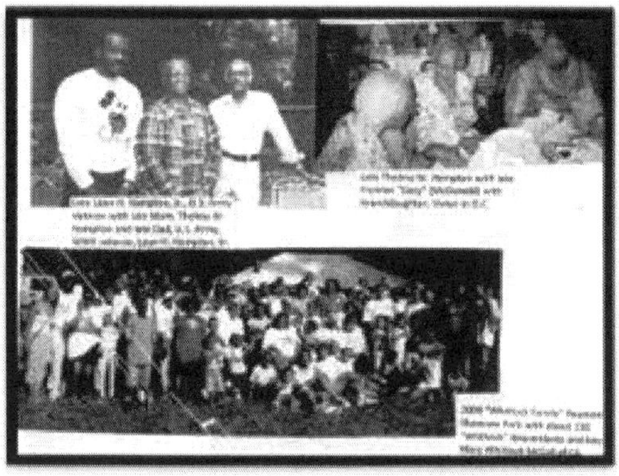

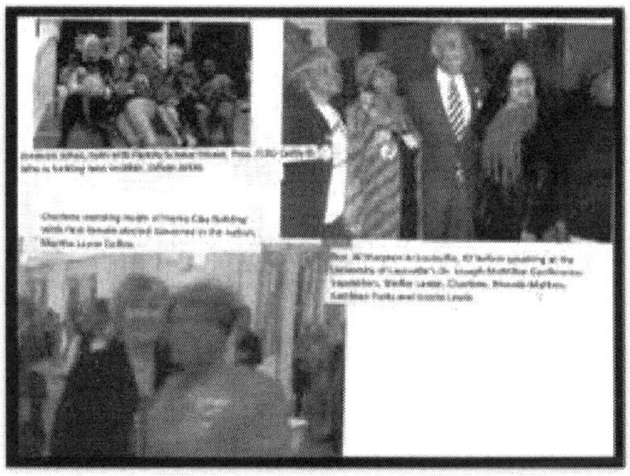

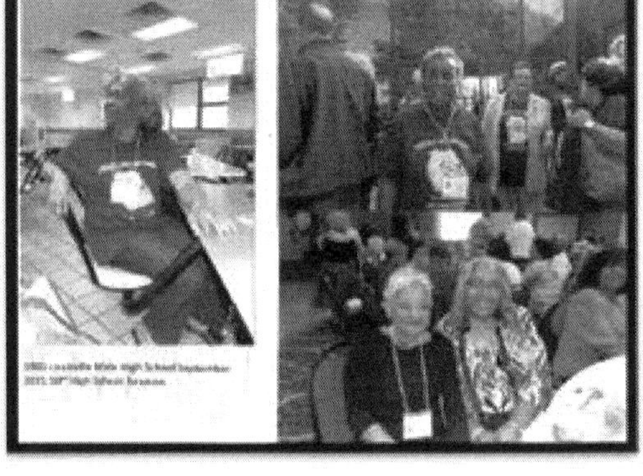

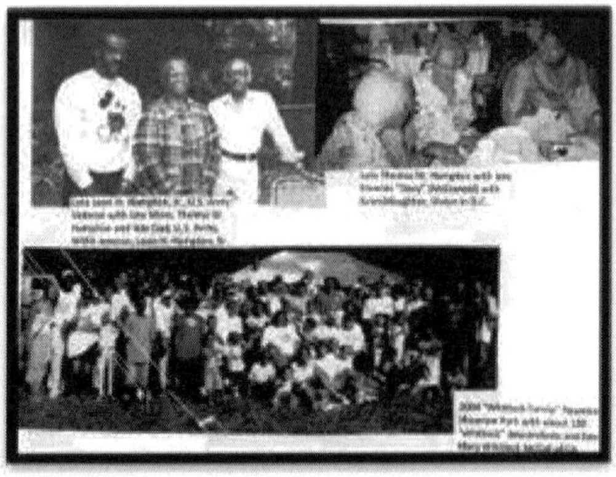

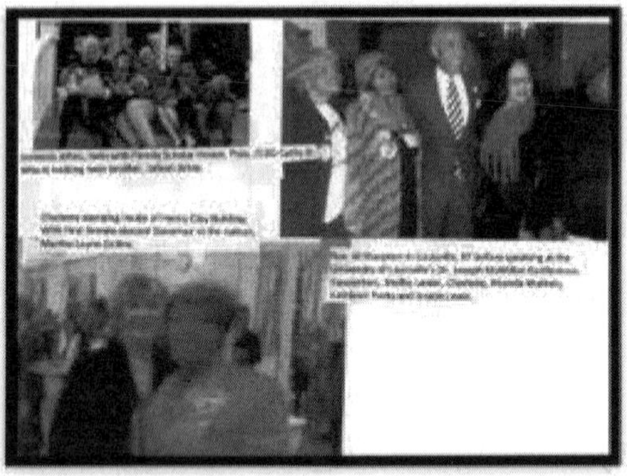

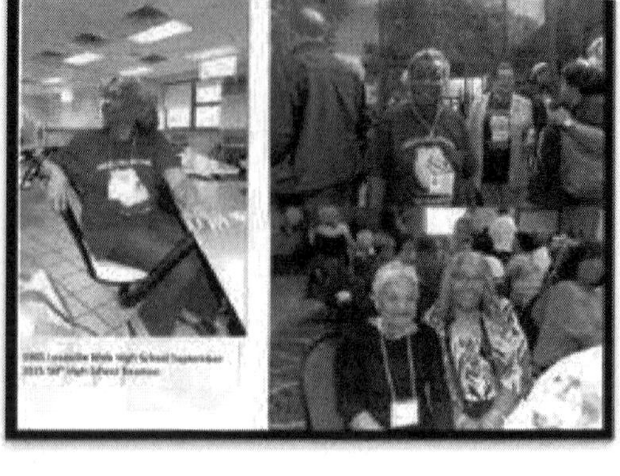

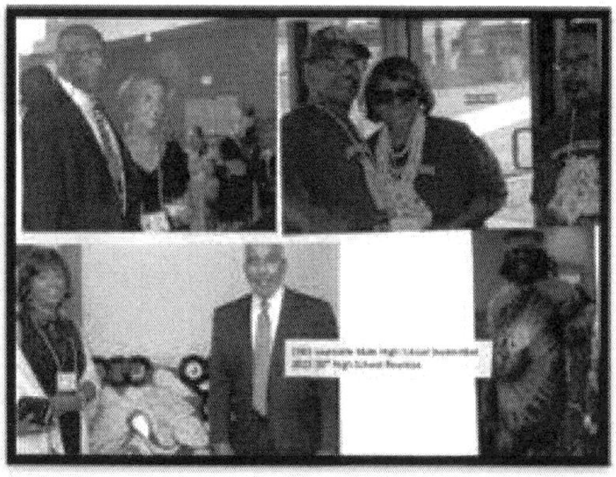

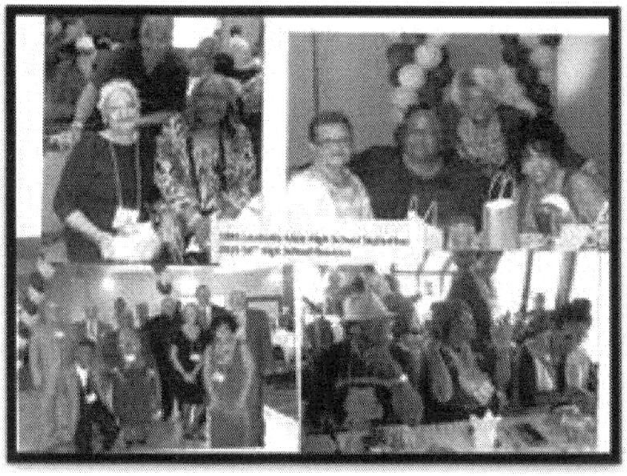

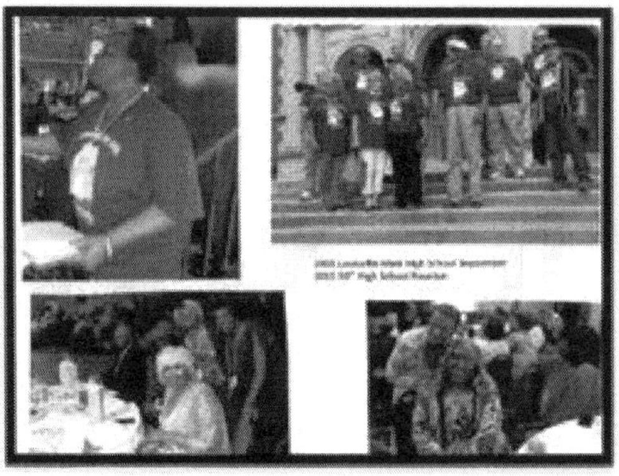

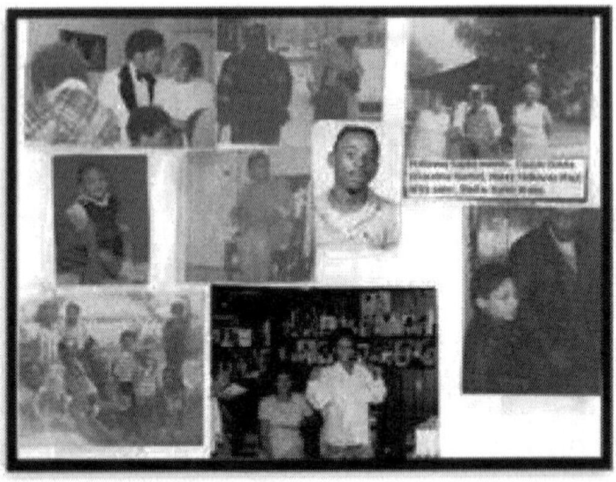

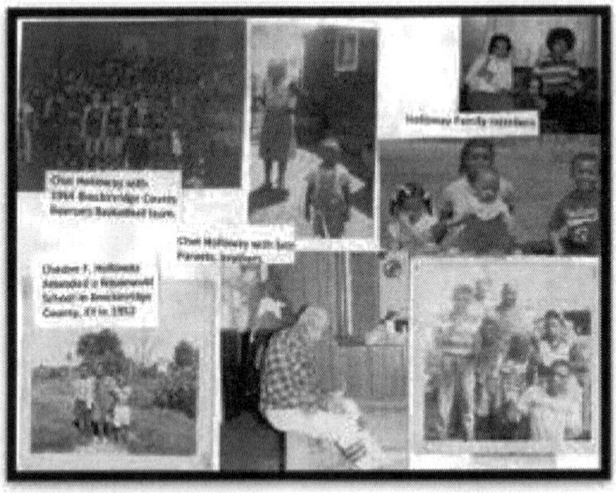

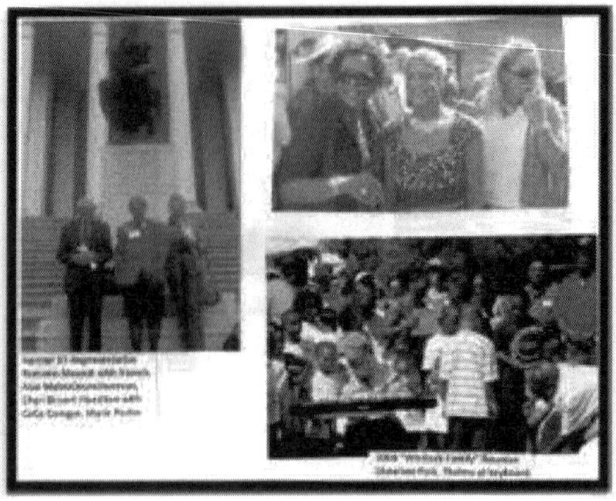

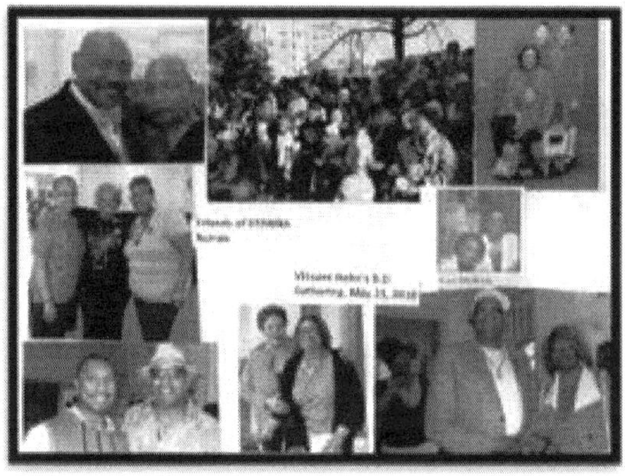

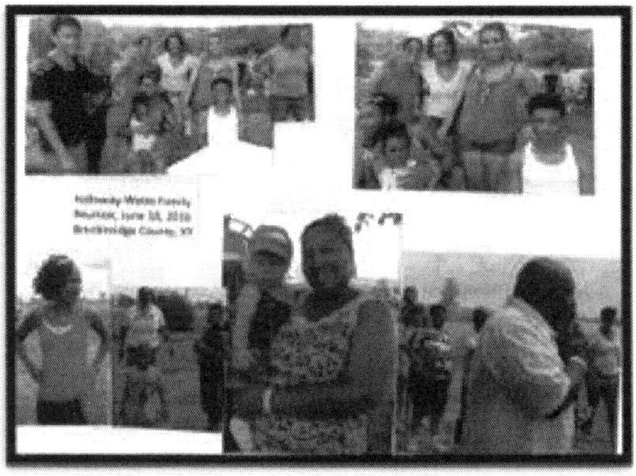

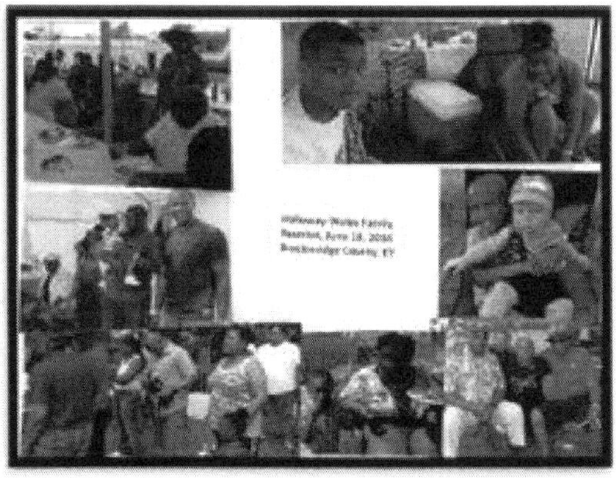

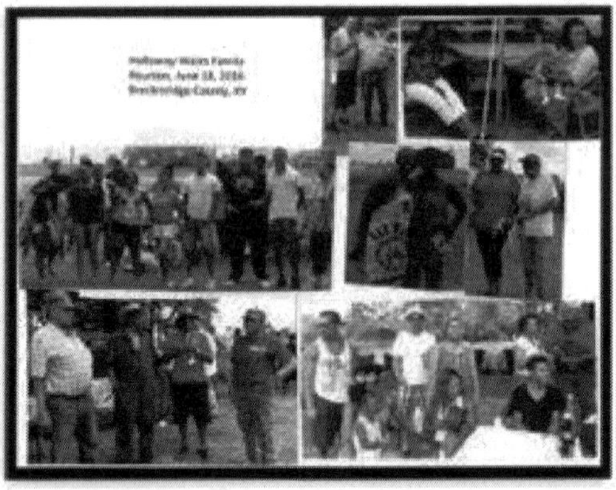

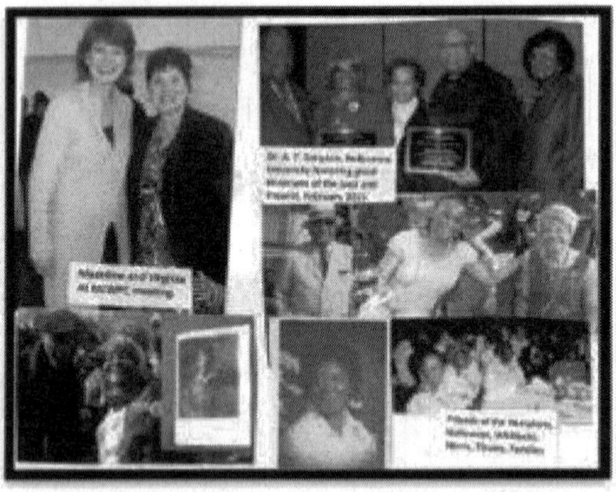

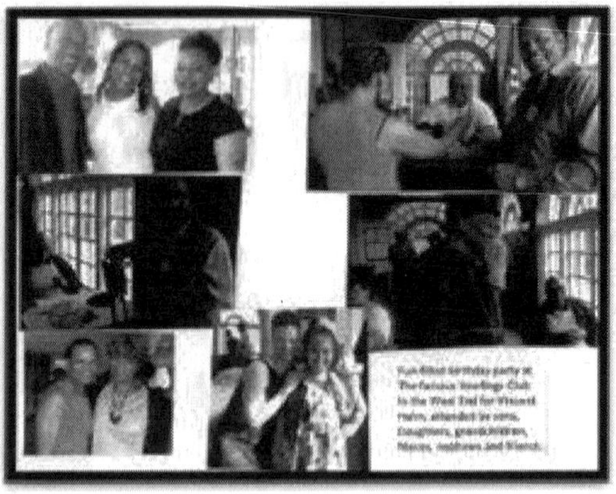

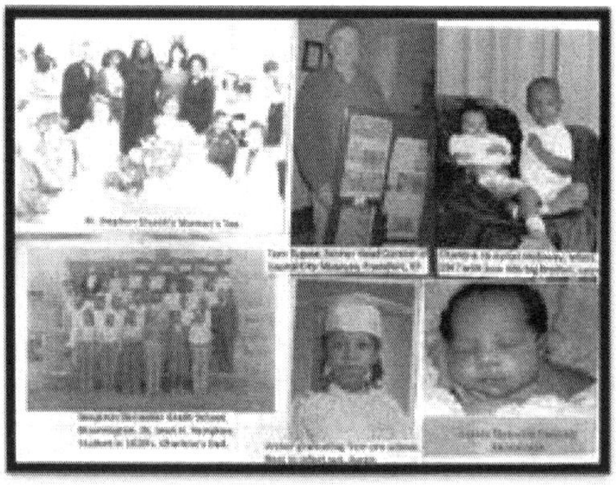

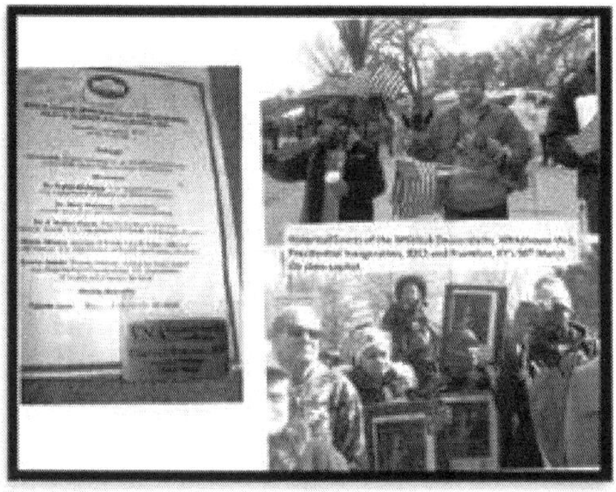

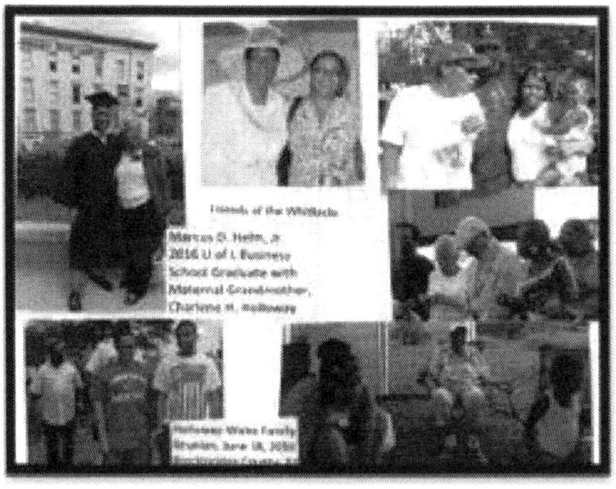

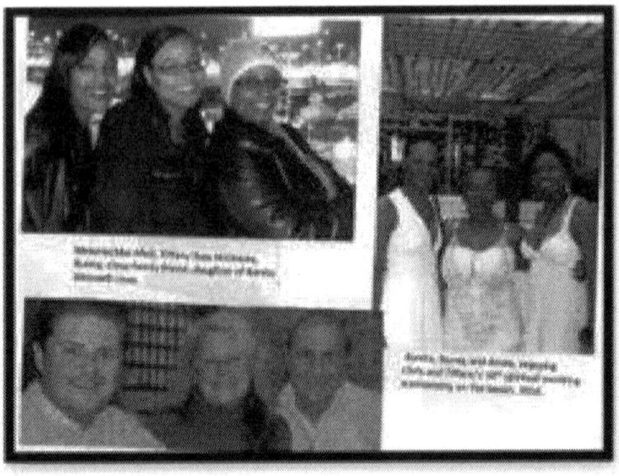

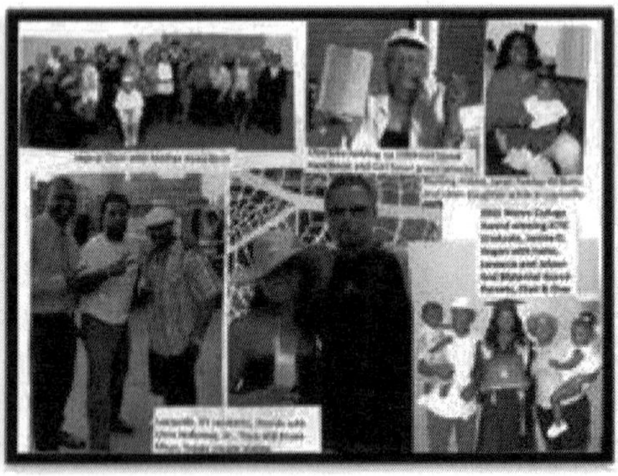

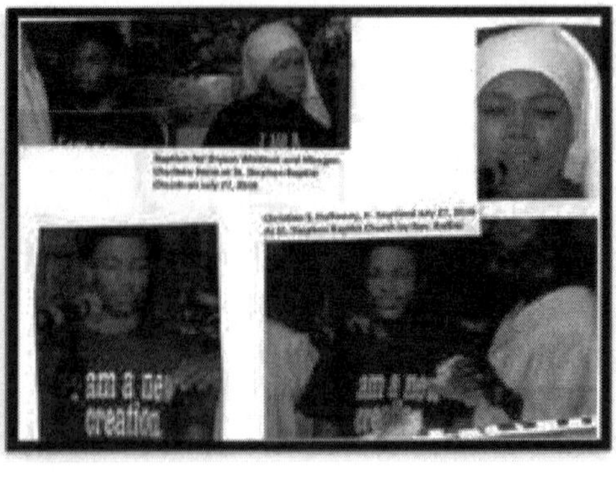
am a new
creation

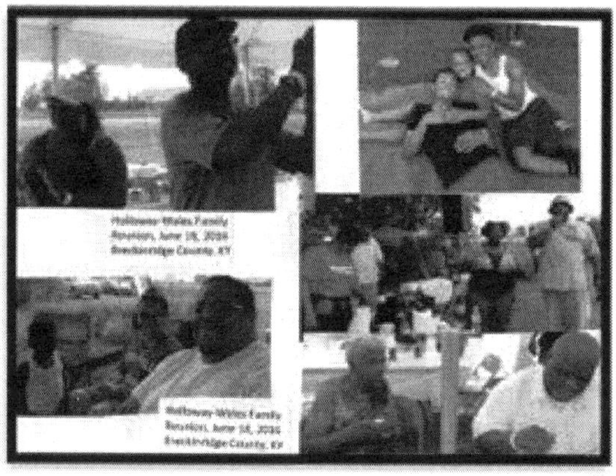

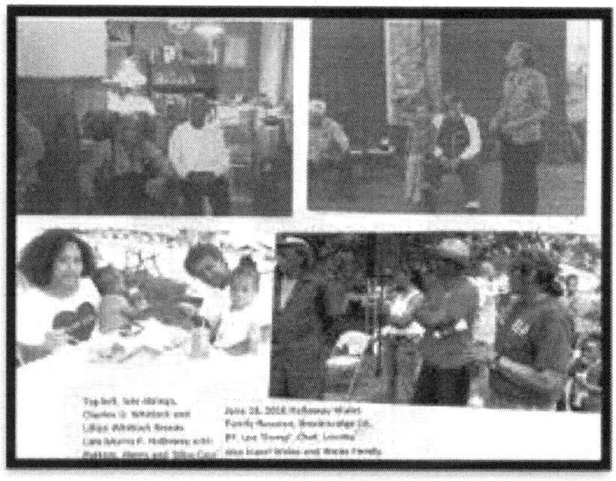

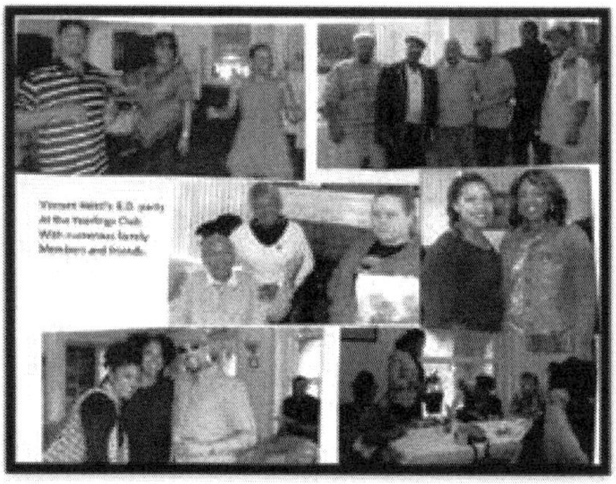

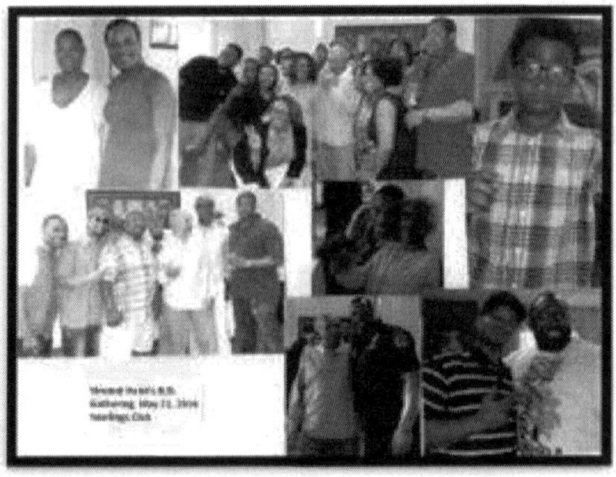

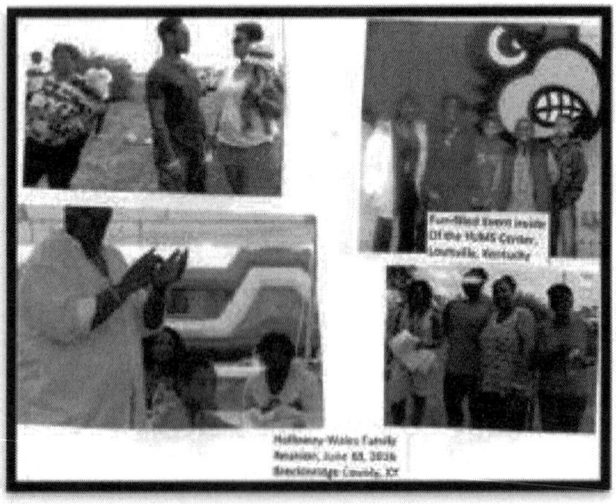

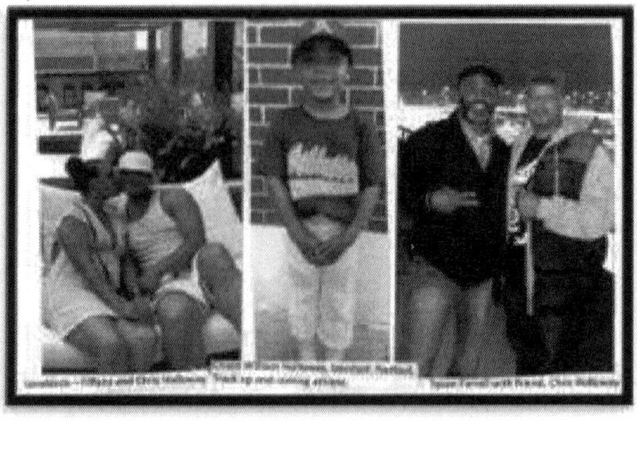

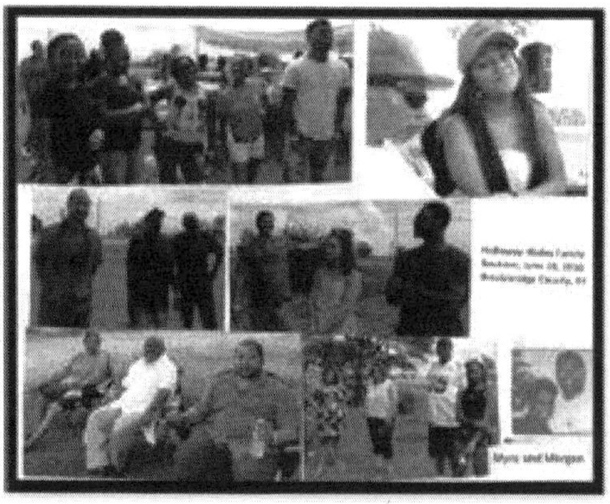

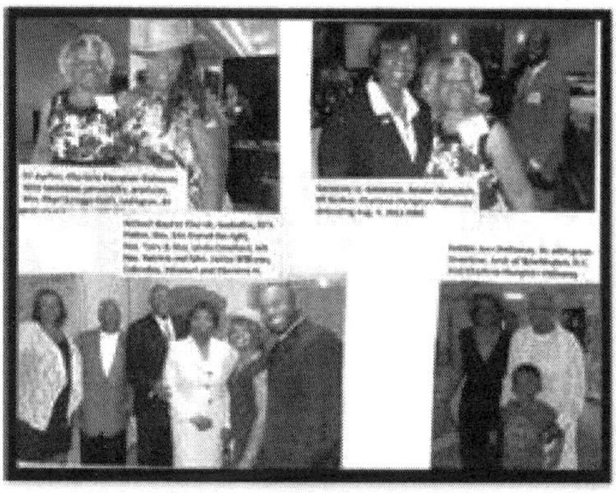

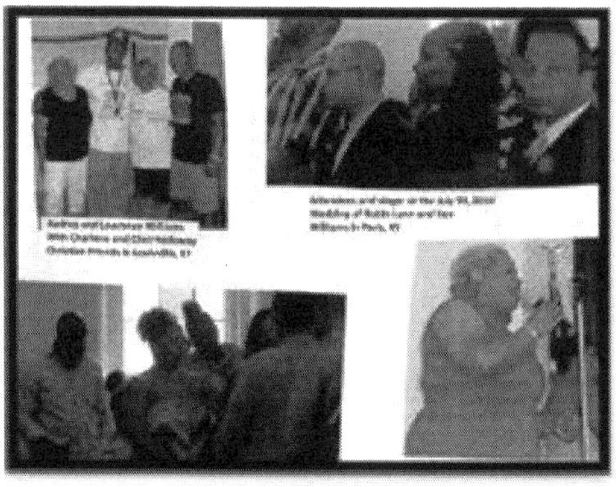

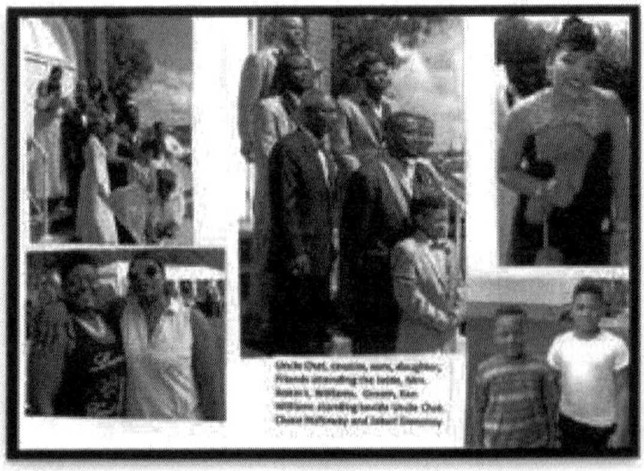

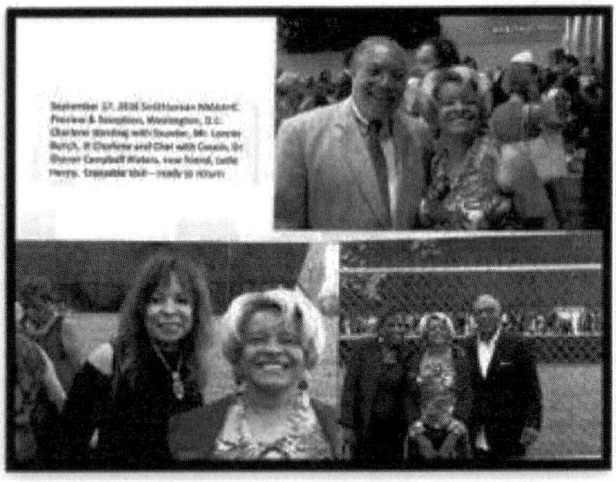

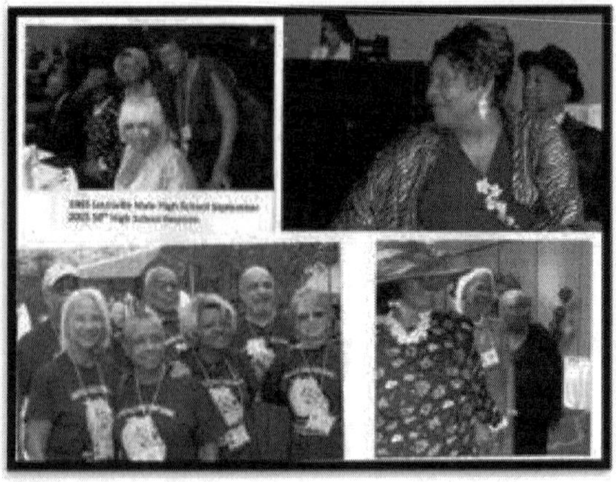

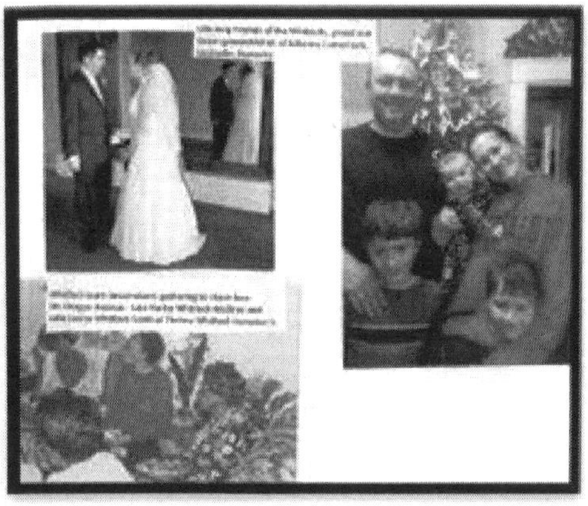

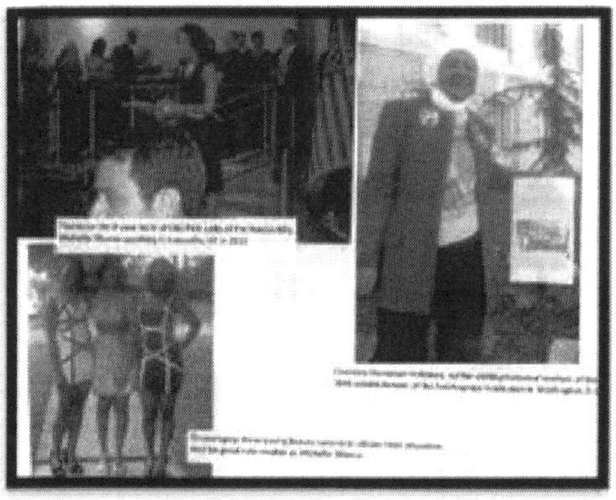

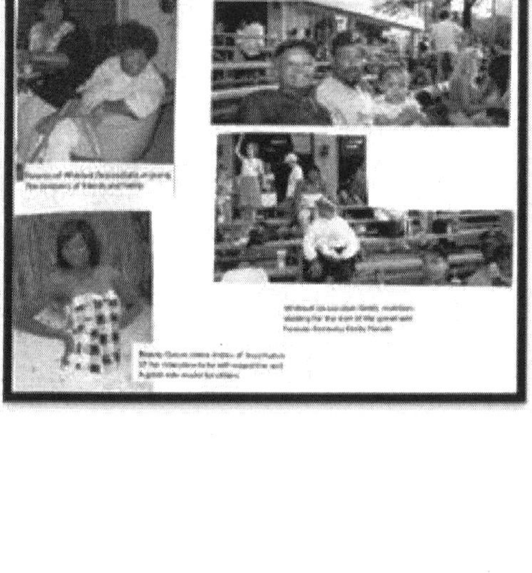

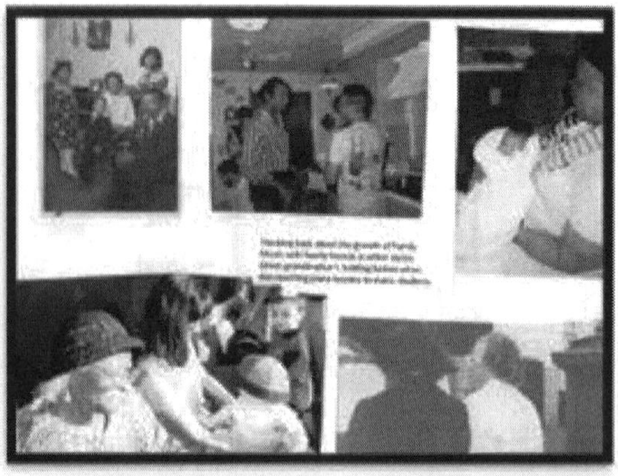

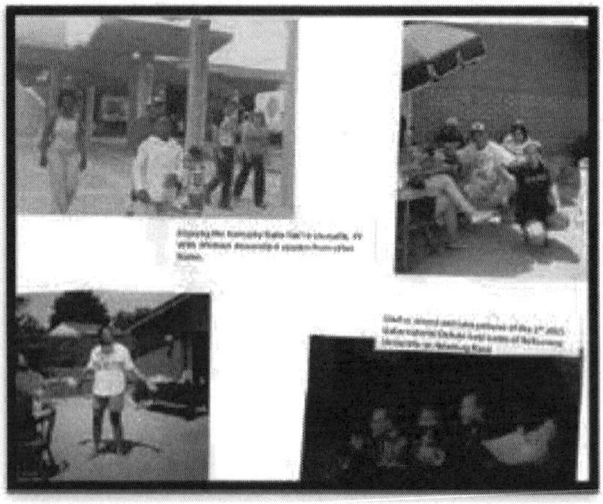

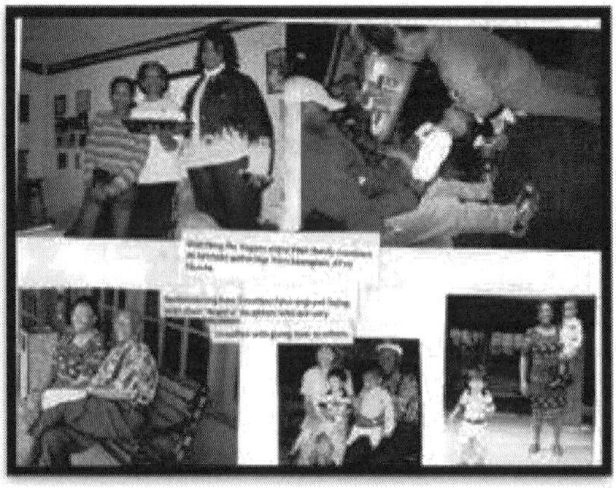

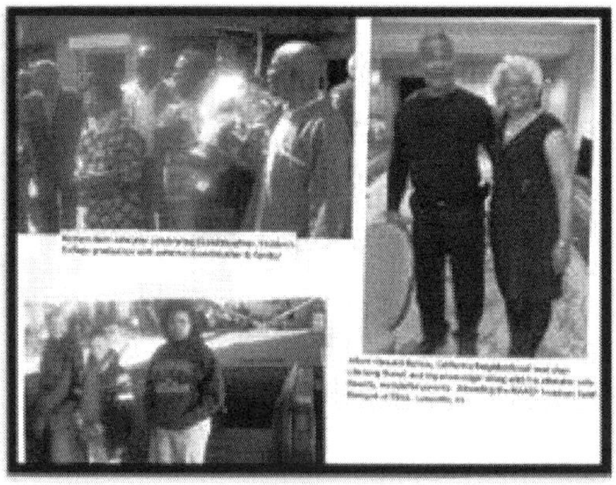

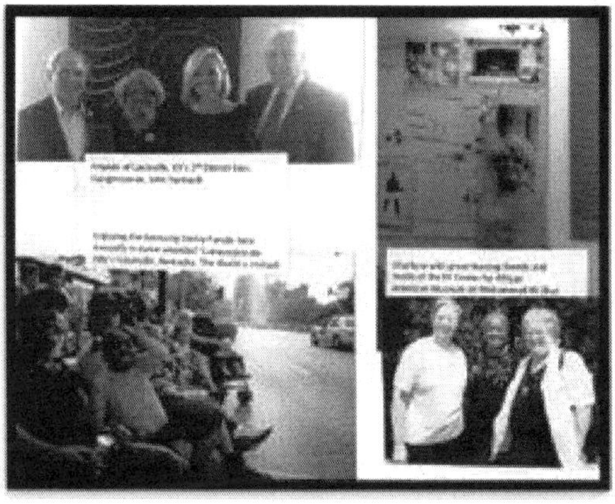

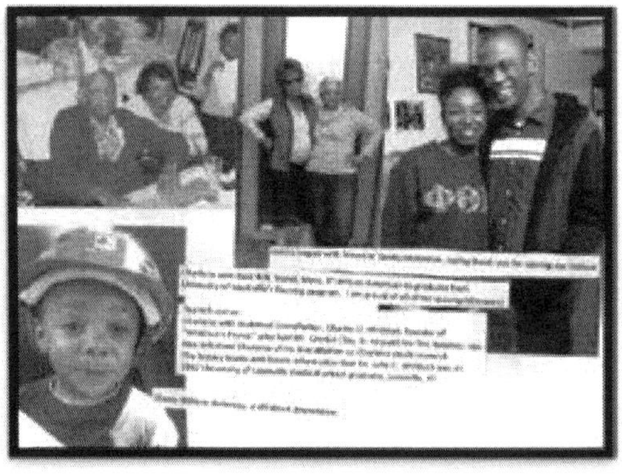

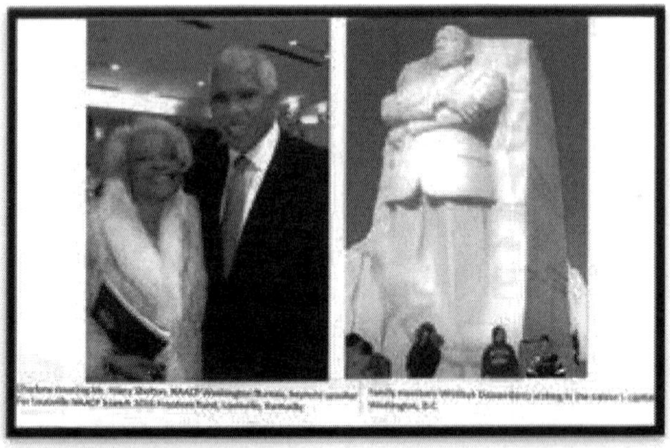

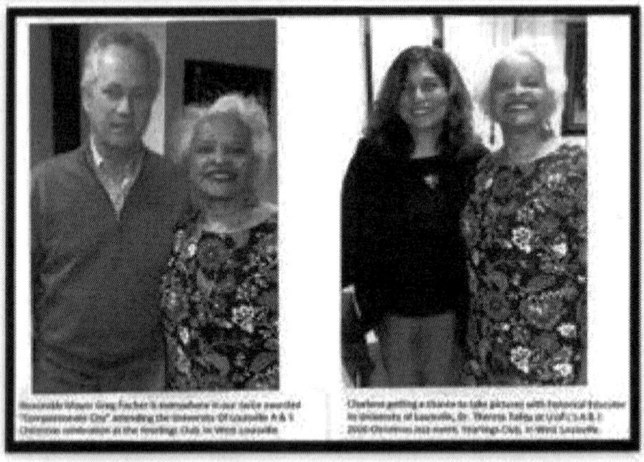

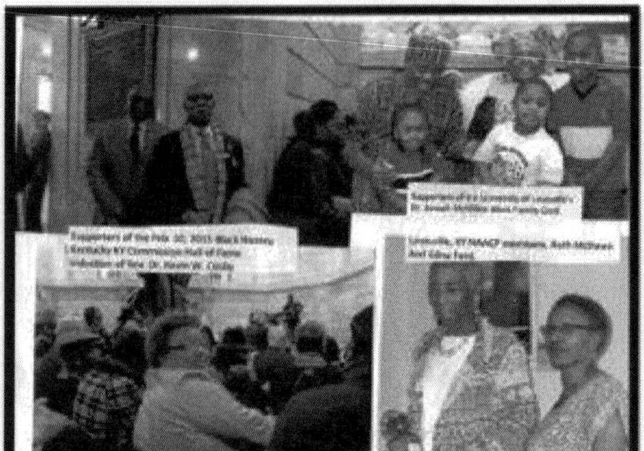

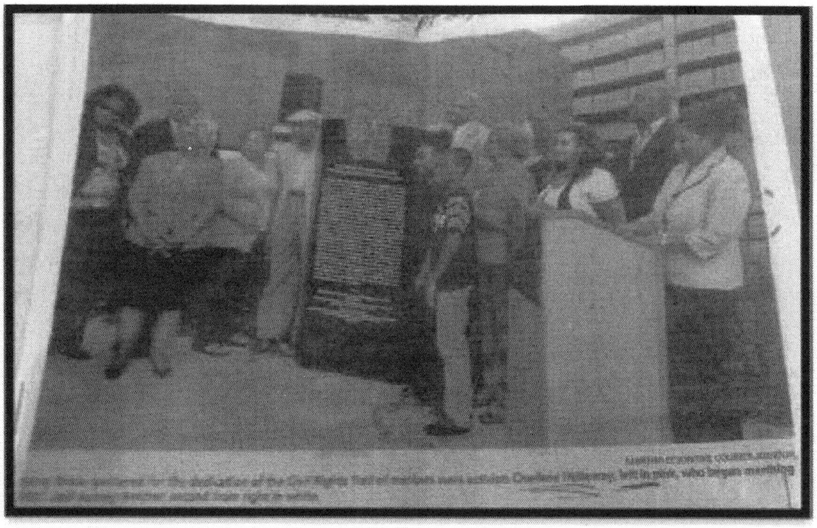

Chapter 11

Mildred and David worked hard together saving their money and caring for their children. As their children began to grow older, David thought long and hard about the future of his family. After careful consideration and praying about their future, David asked Mildred if she would consider moving to Atlanta, Georgia. He wanted to continue his studies and enter a college that would further his religious and spiritual background. Mildred knew that she would be further away and was hesitant at first because she loved the fact that her sister Thelma and brother-in-law, Leon would drive over to St. Louis on the weekends to visit quite often. She also thought about the fact that she would be further away from her parents and especially, Parthenia who always welcomed Mildred home with open arms. Charles D. had also softened up quite a bit and was always glad to see his daughter Mildred visit and always planted many kisses on his grandchildren. Parthenia enjoyed seeing Davida as well as her namesake, Parthenia. Also, Mildred knew that when she came home at Thanksgiving or Christmas, she would always get to visit with many of her aunties and cousins on her mother and father's sides. Mildred would visit many of her cousins who also would come home for the holiday to visit with their parents or siblings. But being the faithful, hardworking wife and mother that she was, she decided to use her contacts at Homer G. Phillips Hospital and have the staff there assist her in securing a very good nursing job in Atlanta. She and David sold their home and off to Atlanta they went with their two daughters.

Even though Atlanta was a large city, like St. Louis, at the time Mildred's early determination to be able to be as independent as possible presented no problems with driving around the city and finding adequate living situations. For the simple fact that there were not very many colored registered nurses. At that time, she easily found nursing jobs at the hospitals for people of color. This eased David's mind and worries. He worked as a very talented and skilled carpenter helping to build new homes in Atlanta in the late 1950's. He was a whiz and a natural when it came to measuring and building homes, garages, porches, and many wooden structures. He enjoyed seeing all of the prosperous people in Atlanta. Mildred began to enroll her daughters in school. Their first home was located on a section of Peachtree Street. Mildred's daughter, Parthenia, was a tiny youngster who had a small stature just like her maternal grandmother. Davida had the stature of her father and was a very tall toddler. Davida was always verbal in letting everyone know when she wanted to eat. With these youngsters being so close in age, it wasn't very long before Davida was much taller than her older sister, Parthenia, was. Mildred knew her parents yearned to see all their grandchildren at any time, not just holidays. While Parthenia and Davida were out of school for the summer break, Mildred and David filled up their car with goodies, the girls' summer clothes, and the family would head to Louisville, Kentucky.

Parthenia and Davida loved to visit with the maternal grandparents. They visited their father's parents as often as David was able to take them. When Parthenia and Davida visited Louisville, they always wanted to stay with 'Auntie'. They enjoyed seeing 'Gramps' as Charles D. was called by his grandchildren, but they wanted to spend the night at 'Auntie's house where they could run through the house with Charlene. Naturally, the girls enjoyed playing with dolls and dollhouses. During the day if 'Auntie' worked a summer job, as she often did on the school playground area providing recreational activities for children in the neighborhood, all of the

Parthenia would spend a lot of time in their grandparent's side yard playing in the dirt and making mud pies. A few times, Davida was seen eating a mud pie or two. It delighted Charlene to take charge and boss her younger cousins around as though she was much older. The girls did not have to worry about Leon Jr. snatching their dolls or teasing them. He was very quiet, studious, and shy. He simply loved to read, watch cartoons and westerns on television. Leon Jr. spent a lot of quiet time in his grandparent's living room watching television by himself. When Charlene, Parthenia, and Davida felt they had made enough mud pies and sometimes took a few bites, they were strongly encouraged by Parthenia Whitlock to come into the house and head directly to the bathroom for a quick bath. Afterwards, the moment they saw 'Gramps,' Charlene would tell her cousins that it was time to play a game called "Robbing Gramps." Their grandfather would tell his wife to make sure he had plenty of change for him to keep in his pants pockets. He would only laugh when they would come around and announce it was time to play their favorite game. He enjoyed seeing his grandchildren so much and was thankful that his daughter Mildred never denied him and Parthenia the opportunity to spend time with them. So he enjoyed seeing them smile about having a quarter or even fifty-cents. Then they all informed their grandparents that it was time for them to go buy a snowball. Mrs. Marie Crumes had a business on the side of her house selling snowballs. Each of these cousins would call out, "Miss Snowball Lady!" She would be so glad to see the cousins visiting from out of town as well as the ones who lived in the neighborhood. She would always tell them, "Welcome back to the city little cousins". Davida and Parthenia liked being noticed as visitors and always told her she would be getting plenty of business from them each and every day while they were in town. All of the cousins would not spend their entire quarter. They saved at least fifteen cents to return later in the evening to buy another snowball from Mrs. Crumes.

Many days, Grandmother Parthenia would be the elected person to comb all three heads of hair. Leon Sr. usually combed Charlene's as well as kept it washed, but there were a few times that Charlene would agree to allow her grandmother to comb hers. Parthenia and Davida had very thick heads of hair. However, young Parthenia had a very tender scalp. Many times she would ask her grandmother, "Do you have to comb it to the grits?" This meant that she was pleading for her grandmother to comb and brush her very long and coarse hair as gently as possible. Davida and Charlene did not have the long braids that young Parthenia possessed. They would stay outside in the yard playing with as much dirt and making as many mud pies as possible. Truly, when the first four grandchildren of Charles D. and Parthenia look back, they can think about how much fun they had doing simple things in life but enjoying each other's company. It will never be hard to forget how Davida showed her deep love for animals of all kinds. More than once, Davida was caught bringing a stray cat or dog into her grandparent's side yard and quickly place the animal down. Then Davida would quickly go into the kitchen, open up her grandparent's refrigerator and find some food for her shortly adopted animals. As always her grandmother would explain to Davida that they were unable to keep any pets at that time. After Davida returned home to her parents, those pets would still need to be fed and cared for. Also, when Davida's parents returned to Louisville to take the children home, her parents would always remind her that of the few pets at home who were looking forward to her return. This made Davida very happy and when the cousins hugged and kissed each other goodbye, there were not as many tears shed.

Chapter 12

As Thelma and Leon's children began to grow up and excel in school, they began to think about their children's future. They felt the need to obtain as much education as they possibly could before their children became adults. The stress of trying to work fulltime and attend college fulltime took a toll on Leon Sr. He began to have many headaches. He was truly a dedicated nursing attendant at the Veterans Hospital (formerly the Old Nichols Hospital) caring for, lifting, and helping many patients. He soon developed abdominal hernias. Leon entered the Veterans Hospital as a patient and accepted the surgery that the doctors stated they needed to perform. Leon had informed his wife Thelma that he had been a very sick child who kept many colds despite receiving much love from his mother. Leon had explained to Thelma about the time his elementary teacher would allow him to stand behind the warm radiators at school. Leon would have to walk a distance to school and being very poor, his shoes were cheaply made and had thin soles. Leon's feet would certainly be soaking wet when he walked in the snow and rain to school when trying to get an education at the Benjamin Banneker Grade School in Bloomington, Indiana for his start in life. Thelma loved Leon so much that she kept encouraging him to at least take classes in a college part-time until he could obtain enough credits to receive his degree. At one point, Leon obtained his application for nursing school at the Old General Hospital in Louisville, Kentucky to become a registered nurse. Instead, he decided that he would rather Thelma have the opportunity to further her education.

Thelma had a very busy schedule teaching school all day and at times staying late for faculty meetings. During the week after school on some days when she wasn't delivering floral arrangements for her father, she gave private piano lessons in her home. Leon was so proud of his wife's accomplishments and her love for music that he continually kept all of their clothes washed and ironed. His mother, Loras Ellen Gray, taught him to be independent and care for everything he owned so he enjoyed keeping their clothes up to par. He cooked, swept, shopped for groceries, and even took Charlene shopping to keep her wardrobe intact. Leon loved to shop for dresses for Thelma as well, as she was petite and had a fine figure. That made it easy for Leon to purchase pretty clothes for her that would fit her perfectly. Thelma continued to play the piano and organ at Mt. Lebanon Baptist church where they all attended. One Sunday evening when the Whitlocks and Hamptons attended an evening service, as Thelma began to play one of her favorite songs on the piano, "I Surrender All", Charlene and Leon Jr. confessed their love and belief in Jesus and stated their desire to be baptized into full fellowship at Mt. Lebanon. This event made Charles D. and Parthenia cry. Charles D. and Parthenia had continued to be very active members of the church and had taken on the responsibility to pick up many children in the neighborhood. Many children who were members of the church told them about not having transportation to and from church. Charles D. may have been very selective about whom his daughters were to date and marry, but he and Parthenia had a heart as big as the city of Louisville when it came to transporting children to Mount Lebanon. They decided to dedicate their lives to giving many people rides to and from church. In fact, Charles D. began purchasing used station wagons so that he could carry as many people as possible at one time. Often times, Charles D. would make two or three trips back and forth from church services to make sure no one was left standing for a city bus or tried to make sure no one had to walk long distances to and from church.

Charles D. became the Superintendent of Sunday School while Parthenia became president of the Pastor's Aide Society. That meant that since Charles D. was also a member of the deacon board, he would have to spend many hours inside the church. Parthenia also belonged to one of the missionary circles that met at different member's homes. When these ladies met, they would sing, pray and discuss the sick and shut-in members of the church whom they had visited since their last meeting. Parthenia and Charles D. took their positions in church very seriously. In fact, they spent very little time participating in activities outside the church.

Charles D. would sometimes awaken very early on a Saturday morning and meet some of his co-workers such as Mr. Finley at the post office or a good church deacon like Mr. Fred Kirby. Together they drove to another county with plenty of woods to go squirrel hunting. Also at times, Charles D. would take Leon Jr. along and invite Leon Sr. to hunt rabbits when rabbit-hunting was in season. But the real sport that Charles D. cherished was fishing. He and Parthenia would at times drive to the Kentucky Lake in Gilbertsville, Kentucky and stay in the Benberry's cabins. It was unheard of for people of color to have their own area of resort with cabins and beds equipped with stoves and many luxuries of the home in various parts of the country. Charles D. had begun acquainted with the Benberry's on one of their prior trips when they had slept in their station wagon. Many times Charles D. and Parthenia would love to go to the banks of the Ohio River to just cast out a line at the edge of Fourth and River Road. Many times Leon Sr. would meet them there after he left work. Charlene began to learn to cast her reel and quickly began to catch a lot of fish. Leon Jr. seemed to not have the patience to sit and wait for a bite from a fish and he would quickly start throwing rocks into the water. Charlene would always tease him and say that he was jealous because she caught more fish than him. Charles D. would make a big deal out of the fish that Charlene caught. Soon Charles D. and Parthenia could hardly make a trip to Kentucky Lake without taking Leon Jr. and Charlene. Charles D. and Parthenia watched their spending closely. Regardless of how much he made at the post office and how much profit he made from his florist business, if any, he did not believe in wasting a penny. Many times Charles D. would buy food and snacks for the family members at nearby stores at the lake. Charlene and Leon Jr. were always happy to eat a can of beanie weenies. For the biggest thrill for them was to watch 'Gramps' hang a big one. 'Gramps' would have a habit of backing his station wagon up to the edge of the lake. Even though there were very large rocks and stones this was a scary moment for Charlene and Leon Jr. They quickly learned to ask 'Gramps' if they could get out of the car before he backed into one of his favorite spots. Charlene and Leon Jr. enjoyed fishing out of the lake but they didn't want to be fished out of the lake. Charles D. was very careful. He never meant to harm his wife or grandchildren. He only wanted to get as close to the water as possible so that he could hear the bells on his reels and rods go off at night just in case he had hung a big one. Many times this is exactly what happened. Charles D. was truly a great fisherman along with Leon Sr. Also, Parthenia was a great fisher lady and Charlene was aspiring to be even better than her grandmother.

Chapter 13

While Charles D. and Parthenia's flower business was flourishing, Thelma continued to teach school and went directly to the home of her parents. She would greet her children and remind them of the importance of making good grades and studying. Thelma continued to help Charles D. deliver his floral arrangements. They were truly a close-knit family who believed in helping each other. Parthenia never allowed Thelma to come home and cook. Parthenia would somehow take a break from helping Charles D. during the day and start a hefty meal. Charles D. was a big man with a hearty and very healthy appetite. Parthenia had learned to prepare many delicious dishes. She always insisted that Thelma sit down to eat dinner before they began to make their deliveries. In many ways, this helped Thelma to make sure her two children were well fed. Since Leon Sr. worked the second shift at the Veterans Hospital, Thelma was not depriving him of the opportunity to be together immediately after she came home from work. Thelma knew that her husband had learned to cook by his careful observations of teaching instructions from his mother, Loras, when she would come to visit Leon Sr. and his family.

Charlene always looked forward to her paternal grandmother's visits. Her grandmother Loras never worried about combing Charlene's hair since Leon Sr. had always done a superb job of that. She and Charlene sat on the porch of Leon Sr.'s home and played jacks. Charlene delighted in having her grandmother Loras teach her to develop hand-eye coordination for the game. After her grandmother Loras left to return to Ohio with Charlene's Aunt Gladora, Charlene would quickly ask her parents if she could walk across the alley to play with the neighbor children. John and Mary Alice Burton had moved into the large house across the alley. They had four children named Michael, Denise, Phyllis, and Tony. After a few months passed, Mrs. Burton gave birth to David. Charlene loved to share her dolls with the Burton girls. She also loved to play school and games with Michael and Tony. When it was time for her to go home, Tony would begin to cry and say, "Taheen, please don't go home." Leon and Thelma realized that Charlene having the opportunity to play with the Burton children kept her from being lonely. As Charlene did not enjoy watching television as her brother Leon did, nor had she learned to recite poems as well as him. Within the next four years, John and Mary Alice were proud parents of two more sons, and another daughter. Their names were James Patrick, Albert Howard, and Alice respectively. Thelma and Leon laughed at how excited Charlene was at each of their arrivals home from the hospital. She knew she now had eight playmates. The family who lived on the other side of Leon and Thelma were the Mortons. Lois and George Morton had a larger family than the Hamptons. There was Barry, Norman, Miriam, and the youngest was Linda Patricia. Since the Burtons were Catholics, the Hamptons were Baptist and the Mortons were Methodist, all of the neighbors could share their religious beliefs. The differences between their religions never stopped their friendships. When John Burton suffered severe back pain, Thelma and Leon were happy to allow him to crawl into the back of their station wagon and take him to be admitted to a local hospital. Charlene was always happy that there was no iron fence or gate at her home. Several of her schoolmates like Garnett Phelps would come by her house and hear Tony Burton cry about her leaving and Garnett would tease Charlene and call her "Taheen". Even friends like Pat McDade, Pat Strong, and Gwen Smith would laugh about Garnett teasing Charlene.

By the time that Leon Jr. was completing his elementary education, Charles D. had taught him to recite many poems. On the night of his graduation from Phillis Wheatley Elementary School, Leon was encouraged by Charles D. to recite the 'Creation'. There was an immediate hush from the audience as Leon began to speak. There were many people in the neighborhood who had attended Phillis Wheatley as children as well as their children. They always came to the Young's Chapel A.M.E. Church where the graduation exercises were held. Charles D. felt that he had inspired Leon not to be shy but to use his God-given talent of speaking.

> Behold, I STAND AT THE DOOR AND KNOCK
> Revelation 3:20
> It was in the cool of evening
> And the Master, I am told
> Sought a place of rest and comfort
> From the elemental cold.
> Sin ruled the house the Master sought,
> Their hearts were hard as rocks.
> They were dwelling in the basement,
> And they couldn't hear Him knock.
> Are you living in the basement?
> Of your heart and mind and soul?
> Are you so sin-fested
> That you've lost your self-control?
> It is later than you think, my friend,
> Just look at life's time-clock.
> Stop living in the basement
> Where you cannot hear Him knock.
> *By Chas. D. Whitlock 12/09/52—2:00a.m.*

Chapter 14

Charles D. and Parthenia kept in touch with their daughter Mildred by phone and by correspondence. Parthenia began to prepare certain dishes for Mildred when she would come home for Thanksgiving. Mildred had been born on Thanksgiving Day and Parthenia delighted in preparing those special dishes for her younger daughter. Mildred would write to Parthenia and Charles D. to inform them that her two daughters were excelling in school. The proud grandparents beamed with pride. They felt they had encouraged the children each and every time they saw them in person or talked to them on the phone. They also knew that Mildred was bound and determined to encourage her children to do well along with their father, David. One special Thanksgiving, Mildred found out late she could not come home for that holiday. Charles D. went to the airport and bought plane tickets for Parthenia, Leon Jr., Charlene and himself. That was a truly memorable Thanksgiving. That was Charlene's first plane ride but not Leon's. He had been given the opportunity only that past summer to fly to San Francisco, California, with Charles D. and Parthenia to visit Charles D.'s brother, Ellis Whitlock and many of his family members. This trip gave Leon Jr. the opportunity to meet many of his cousins in California and Thelma's first cousin, Mary Thelma Whitlock McCall. Little did they know that some forty-odd years later, they would still be communicating by writing and visiting each other.

With Leon Jr. entering middle school and integration beginning at that time in the Old Louisville Public School System, it brought many challenges. Thelma wanted to become more prepared in her educational studies. She and Leon Sr. decided that she would apply and enroll again into Indiana University and attend summer school classes in Bloomington, Indiana. Thelma stayed inside of a dorm or stayed with life-long friends of Leon Sr.'s such as the Maceo Deal family. Leon had very few close family members there in Bloomington at the time. He had a half-sister with ten children who resided in the city, but he had little contact with Mary Frances Brown. His older sister, Gladora Hampton, left Bloomington years before, married the R . Thomas L. Tinsley, and moved to Irvington, Kentucky. The Tinsleys moved away again to the cities of Columbus and Akron, Ohio, respectively. Thelma did not really spend a lot of time visiting relatives and friends in Bloomington. She had her mind set on completing all of the requirements to march and receive her master's degree in Education.

Thelma took time off from playing for many of the choirs that she had taught several classical, spiritual and worshipful songs. She taught them anthems as well. She had begun studying Hymnology at the Southern Baptist Theological Seminary before she left for summer school at Indiana University. She had also taught at least six to eight young males and females to play the piano. Thelma wasted none of her precious time. She truly was interested in young people developing their musical talents. Thelma always encouraged Mary Lois Jackmon to play the piano as often as opportunity allowed. Mary Lois was one of three very obedient daughters of Mr. and Mrs. Lucian Jackmon. This couple always marveled at Thelma's encouragement to have Mary Lois play for church services and for the junior choir.

When Thelma left the first summer, there were a few snide remarks from some very inconsiderate members of the senior choir. Charles D., Parthenia, and Leon Sr. encouraged her not to pay any attention to them. Her parents knew that Thelma hoped to gain more education before her children became adults. Thelma thought about how difficult it was for her to gain a permanent position teaching and how even a supervisor of music instruction in the Old Louisville School System, who was of color, mistreated her. Thelma felt she must increase her credentials. Thelma had a truly difficult time before she started working toward her master's degree as well as after she received that degree. Thelma had accepted a permanent position teaching kindergarten as her first full-time position only to have it snatched from under her and the position was given to the principal's wife. Thelma had dazzled the kindergarten classes with her expertise of playing so many happy songs. With music being the universal language, how could she go wrong by delighting the children with excellent musical selections.

Before Thelma had completed all of her courses for her master's degree, her mother suddenly suffered a massive stroke. Parthenia remembered she had an older sister, Emma, a large woman of stature who suffered from high blood pressure and who died from a fatal stroke. Parthenia was a woman who weighed less than a hundred pounds. She certainly did not have the appetite that Charles D. had acquired. Mildred was summoned to bring her nursing skills and expertise to inquire about what other medical procedures could be done for Parthenia. Parthenia's attending physician had given her up to die. Mildred would not accept the physician's decision to give up. Mildred began to call several other doctors in the city until she found a young Dr. Moses who referred Parthenia to a fine neurologist name Dr. Roseman. He would come out to visit Parthenia at her house after she was discharged from the Old Red Cross Hospital. He encouraged Charlene to buy rubber balls that could fit into her grandmother's hand. He had Charlene to instruct her grandmother to have her open and close her hands while gripping the balls. Little did the Whitlock family and Charlene know that this was actually a part of physical therapy. Parthenia's speech was sorely affected. One day as her sister Mollie was there to visit, Mollie began to cry. She stated to Charlene and Leon Jr. that she wished she were her sick rather than Parthenia. Mollie went on to tell Charlene and Leon Jr. of how Parthenia and Charles D. looked after she and their baby sister, Laura, when they were kids. Mollie said that she had no children or grandchildren. Her husband had left her for another woman. Many people prayed for the Whitlock family and Parthenia. She had been instrumental in participating in numerous organizations at Mt. Lebanon Baptist Church. Leon offered his love and kindness to Thelma. He knew just how much Thelma loved both of her parents. As he had lost his mother only the year before and Thelma joined he and Charlene at Loras Ellen Gray's funeral in Akron, Ohio.

Leon reminded Charlene that he could never forget how she told her dad that he could have all of her sixty some odd dollars in her savings account at the T-Bar-V Savings Ranch where she and Leon Jr. had begun to save for emergencies and help both of them to prepare for their future. Charlene gave all but five dollars to her dad to help pay for the expenses of her paternal grandmother's funeral cost.

As Parthenia was blessed to recover from her stroke, Thelma realized that she actually had enough credits to obtain her master's degree. With Parthenia's health returning, she, Charles D., Leon Sr., Leon Jr., and Charlene attended the ceremonies on the campus of Indiana University to witness Thelma marching and carrying out her wishes and goals to further her education.

Chapter 15

Mildred began to teach practical nursing students while she was living in Atlanta, Georgia. She began working at the Grady Hospital in the city. She and David who was completing his degree in a religious school decided that it was time for them to increase their family. Mildred had left a job as the infirmary nurse on the campus of Spelman College. She and David were hoping that maybe they would be a given son. On May 6, 1957, Mildred delivered a sweet little baby girl whom she named after her only sister, Thelma. She gave Thelma the middle name of Parthenia's sister; Louise who was next to Parthenia in age. This baby girl was named Thelma Louise, but she was given the nickname of 'Peaches' due to the fact that she was born in the state of Georgia. She was also called Wee-One or Weasy at times. There had not been a Whitlock grandbaby for several years, so everyone was ecstatic over Thelma Louise's birth. Mildred had been so instrumental in obtaining a Neurologist for her mother. She made it her business to drive home to Louisville every few months when weather permitted. Parthenia began to speak better, and her former doctor told Charles D. that her recovery had been a miracle as far as he was concerned. As Parthenia had been very sick and was told she was on death's door. But with the magnanimous nursing that Mildred had brought to her mother, Parthenia after Mildred was summons to return to Louisville.

There was little doubt that her presence played a very large portion of Parthenia's determinedness to recover to speak, eat, walk again as well as her ability to resume many of her previous activities. Parthenia at times felt that Charles D. working in his florist business and working at the post office was overwhelming for her. At times, she would call Mildred and tell her that she wanted to visit her. One on occasion; when Charlene was twelve years old, Parthenia decided that she wanted Charlene to accompany her to Atlanta. After all, Charlene had worked with her grandmother to help her regain strength in her hands and arms. Parthenia also told Charlene, that it meant so much to her when she would come by her house every morning opening her blinds and smiling at her. Parthenia had begun to call Charlene her 'Sunshine.' Thelma, Leon Sr., and Charles D. agreed to send Charlene to Atlanta with Parthenia. They left the Union Train Station at 10th & Broadway riding in a Pullman. This was a wonderful and fulfilling trip for both Parthenia and Charlene. This gave them the opportunity to spend some very special time to be together as grandmother and granddaughter. To their surprise, one of the wonderful deacons of the church, Mr. Aaron Brown was working on the train. Mr. Brown made sure that Parthenia and Charlene ate adequately by treating them to many meals. Mr. Brown knew that Parthenia was a loving and kind Christian woman, who had been a major role player in helping to build and maintain a very large congregation at Mt. Lebanon. He also knew that the Whitlocks had given him and his wife rides home at times from church. Parthenia immensely enjoyed her visit with Mildred and her family. Of course, Charlene always enjoyed being with her cousins and had the opportunity to cuddle Wee-One.

After several weeks of visiting with Mildred and her family, Parthenia returned to Louisville with Charlene by her side. Parthenia began to drive again and talked with Charles D. about the fact that maybe it was time for him to retire from the post office. Then they could focus on their florist business and could spend more time on the fishing banks. Not long after that, Charles D. retired from the post office. The day he left, he could not help but cry. He thought back about all the years that he had always tried to never miss a day of work, and how he used his hard-earned money to help his daughters enter into college. He also thought about all of the friends that he made. He also thought about how he helped many younger workers retain their jobs by counseling them when they had personal problems. He also thought about the co-workers who read his poetry; as well as, those who shared their poetry with him. One such friend was named Mr. Jarman; who Charles D. not only gave rides to and from work, but encouraged him to develop his talents of writing poetry.

Parthenia was elated that she and Charles D. were able to spend more time together. Charles D. took Parthenia to the doctor weekly to make sure that she received her injections of medication to keep her blood pressure within normal limits. They began to make more trips to Kentucky Lake to go fishing. They also went to the banks of the Ohio River at Fourth and River Road more often. One night after Parthenia decided that they were doing more of feeding the fish than catching them, they decided to drive to a nearby fish restaurant. In that era of time, people of color were expected to walk to the back door of the restaurant and ask for their order of fish, pay for it with their money and eat the fish either in their car or elsewhere other than inside of the restaurant. Charlene began to question Parthenia and Charles D. as to why would we have to be treated in this manner, and what had we done to be treated this way. They only responded in a kind way. To try to explain that people of color were not accepted inside many places, because it was thought that they would not know how to act and that also people of color had not been given certain equal rights. It just didn't make any sense to Charlene.

Charles D. and Parthenia assured Leon Jr. and Charlene that maybe things would get better for people of color. Mildred would call her parents, and tell her about how there had been demonstrations and boycotts of the major stores in Atlanta lead by the Rev. Dr. Martin Luther King, Jr. Charles D. felt that surely there would be a change that would affect people of color in every city in the United States.

Chapter 16

Thelma and Leon knew that while their kids were still young, but old enough to understand historical events, at times they decided to allow them to travel during the spring break. Thelma decided to take Charlene and Leon Jr. with a tour group headed by Mrs. Roberta Masterson, a teacher at DuValle Junior High School. Some children from the California Neighborhood like Eddie Williams as well as sisters, Gloria and Barbara Wheeler would join the group. Some of the young boys who joined the group were Raoul Cunningham, James Mosby, Robert Dockery, and James Bennett. Mrs. Masterson planned an ideal itinerary for about 40 to 60 students and adults. The group would leave Louisville on a train from the old downtown train station and travel to Washington, D.C. This group would tour the nation's capital and see many historical sites, but never stayed in D.C. overnight due to poor accommodations for people of color. After touring Washington, D.C., the group would ride on a chartered bus into New York City and stay in a hotel called Hotel New Yorker. The group had the opportunity to eat at the Automat for quick meals. Charlene and Leon Jr. were so excited about getting a chance to see and climb up the many steps inside of the Statue of Liberty as well as tour the Empire State Building. They also got excited about getting the chance to see the Rockettes perform at Radio City Hall. Thelma, their mother, had told them about her travels, as a young woman, to New York City with her dear friend Gladys Watts.

Thelma would call long distance to Leon Sr., Charles D., and Parthenia to let them know everyone was doing okay and to inquire about them. Thelma even had the opportunity to visit Parthenia's aunt, Lavada Martin, who was Parthenia's mother's youngest sister. Aunt Lavada had moved to New York City in the late 30's from Clarksville, Tennessee, and made that city her home. She would go to the hotel dressed in her lavish fur coats, and Leon Jr. and Charlene were astonished at her northern accent. Also, Thelma, Leon Jr., and Charlene were fortunate enough to visit with Charles D.'s nephew, Dudley Whitlock, Jr. and Charles D.'s sister-in-law Gladys and her two grandchildren David and Lynda. Dudley Sr., an older brother of Charles D.'s had passed away several years before.

After The Louisville tour group visited New York, they would travel by chartered bus to Philadelphia and stay in Father Devine's Hotel. Visiting in Philadelphia gave the group an opportunity to see one of the United States mints, the Liberty Bell as well as the home of Betsy Ross and many other historical sites.

Thelma's children never forgot to bring souvenirs to the family members back home. By the spring of the next year, Thelma and Leon Sr. had enough money saved for Thelma and her children to take another tour with Mrs. Masterson. Leon Jr. and Charlene were proud that they had sold seeds and Christmas cards to have their own spending money for this trip. This time the trip included Boston, Massachusetts. The tour group was able to see Plymouth Rock and many other sites. Leon Jr. and Charlene felt they were two of some of the luckiest kids in the neighborhood.

When the summer came, Leon Jr. and Charlene were always ready to ride to Kentucky Lake with Parthenia and Charles D. Also both were delighted when their cousins from Georgia would visit during the summer. Off they would go to the Snowball Lady, Mrs. Marie Crumes, for their snowballs. They knew these fun times would be something to talk about in later years.

Thelma continued giving private piano lessons in her home on Saturdays and sometimes during the week. She was so fond of some of her piano students like Marshall Kaufman, Elizabeth Mae Brown, Roberta Medlock and Phyllis Jean. Thelma, at times, would stay up late at night on Fridays playing the piano and singing with her dear friend, Cascilla Springer. When Leon Sr. would come in from work after midnight, riding the bus or sometimes paying one of his co-workers for a ride home, he would be amazed at how long those two could play and sing for hours. At times he would join in and sing a few songs with them. The three of them knew what a Mighty God we serve!

Thelma was also initiated into Sigma Gamma Rho Sorority during this time. She met with her chapter and allowed her sorors to meet in her home and discuss their abilities to assist young people to further their education and obtain their degrees at various colleges. Due to her very busy schedule of giving piano lessons, teaching school at either Jackson Junior High or Booker T. Washington Elementary, and assisting her father, Charles D. with his floral business and playing for Mt. Lebanon Baptist Church, Thelma had little time to meet on a regular basis with her sorors. Leon Sr. never complained about her busy schedule. He learned early in their marriage that it was meant to be that their marital time would be shared with many other people. He actually marveled at how well so many of her students like Jean and Patsy Ford easily learned to play the piano and played at many school functions as well as church services. Roberta Medlock played for her high school graduation exercises as well in Chicago, Illinois. Somehow Leon realized that Thelma would probably be a legend of a musician always willing to teach, play, and go the extra mile so that others could follow her lead, share their musical talents and one day even write scores to be published and sung by many people throughout the United States.

About two years later, Charlene began to become interested in the American Civil Rights movement and requested permission from her parents to join in the marches. Even though she was attending the Henry B. Manly Junior High School, and was only thirteen years of age, it did not stop her from needing to do her share so that people of all colors, race, creed, and cultures could receive equal rights. Thelma, Leon Sr., Charles D., and Parthenia would make sure Charlene always had a few dollars and change in her pockets in case the restaurants or movie theaters agree to open their doors to the demonstrators. After Charlene was arrested the first time, April 18, 1961, Charles D., Parthenia and Thelma came to get her after she was allowed a phone call to be released. Leon Jr. had become concerned about his younger sister and also joined the American Civil Rights marches and he too was arrested the same day but from a deli at the corner of Fifth & Chestnut Street. After one of the ministers announced that all participants must be of high school age to join the marches, Charlene began to cry on the shoulder of her minister, Rev. Dr. Frederick G. Sampson. He informed the minister who made that announcement that Charlene had been an active and peaceful participant even at the age of thirteen. She had already been arrested for her prior participations. Leon Sr. would call from his second shift job to make sure that his son and daughter were okay. Charlene and Leon Jr. participated in the sit-ins and squat-ins. All of the demonstrators were peaceful and quiet.

Even though Charlene's homeroom teacher overheard some of her classmates talk about Charlene's involvement in the marches, she was unable to keep Charlene after school one day long enough to miss meeting Dr. Martin Luther King, Jr. Charlene was able to tell her parents and grandparents how she walked to the podium of the historic Quinn Chapel A.M.E. Church on Chestnut Street, shook Dr. King's hand, looking him in the eyes and thanked him for coming to Louisville, Kentucky, to help to assist in the peaceful marches for all people's rights. That summer in June, 1961, Charlene would be arrested again but had turned fourteen years of age, when she peacefully held up a sign at an amusement park in the West End of the city near Shawnee Park.

Chapter 17

Mildred visited her parents as often as possible. She continued to work along with her husband David and rear their three daughters. David continued his studies in a college of Divinity. Mildred and David were surprised to find out that in late 1960, she became pregnant and expected their fourth child. She worked throughout her pregnancy nursing many sick until she went into labor and delivered their son, David Furnace Harris, Jr. born August 3, 1961. Mildred was so delighted that she could bear a son for her husband. It was important to him that he would have a son to carry on the family name. Parthenia could hardly wait to visit Mildred and her new arrival. Parthenia and Charlene took a flight to Atlanta as soon as Thelma and Charles D. could arrange it. Of course when Charlene arrived in Atlanta, not only was she eager to see the new baby cousin, but she was always eager to see her cousins Parthenia, Davida, and Thelma Louise (Wee-One).

The next spring, Thelma decided that she had saved enough money for her sister Mildred to travel with Mrs. Roberta Masterson during the spring school break. Thelma paid for Mildred, her three daughters, Charlene, and Leon Jr. to join the tour group. Thelma decided to stay home and help with Mildred's new baby along with Parthenia. They naturally toured Washington, D.C., New York, and Philadelphia but this year the tour headed to Quebec, Canada. This was a delightful and educational trip for everyone. Of course, Mildred and all of the children received a visit to the Hotel New Yorker from Aunt Lavada, who always wore her lavish furs. This indeed kept the family close and would prove in later years that each could call one another in the time of trouble or need.

Years later, the cousins and aunties would talk about their trips and how much it meant to all of them. Mildred's daughters, who were old enough to remember the trip, have never stopped praising Auntie for her unselfish way of affording them that trip. They felt as blessed as Charlene and Leon and felt they were some of the most blessed kids in their neighborhood. Parthenia and Charles D. knew they had instilled in their daughters to share not only their love but their earnings as well. Many times the cousins visited each other and enjoyed many happy times together.

At various times, David and Mildred continued to take all four of their children to San Antonio, Texas, his hometown, to visit family members. David had several brothers and a sister, named Dorothy, whom all of his children were fond of. Those visits gave young Parthenia, Davida, young Thelma, and David, Jr. the opportunity to know and play with their cousins in Texas as well.

Mildred was also interested in the American Civil Rights marches and demonstrations to promote integration. She always took her children, niece, and nephew to visit many parks and recreational facilities no matter which city she lived in. When the opportunity presented itself, Mildred headed to Washington, D.C. to join the great historical march lead by Rev. Dr. Martin Luther King, Jr. on August 28, 1963. She had hoped to see her nephew, Leon Jr. who turned nineteen years old that day. He had been an American Civil Rights peaceful protester beginning in 1961 at age 16 years in Louisville, KY. The multitude of people who gathered for that grand and historical march would prove to be impossible for Mildred and Leon Jr. to communicate with each other until they returned to their own cities and spoke by phone. For years to come, her participation in that march made her feel really proud. Leon Jr. felt the same way with getting a ticket through businesswoman, Mrs. Dann C. Byck in order to ride the bus to that historic march.

Charles D. had continued to keep in touch with his brothers and sisters. His sister, Lillian lived on Gallagher Street one door from his sister-in-law Mollie while his younger sister, Ethel moved to the area of Newburg with her husband Louis Frierson. Charles D. and Parthenia would visit Ethel and Louis in their home at 4109 St. Charles Lane. Charles D. even visited his brother Ellis in California taking Parthenia and Leon Jr. with him. When his sister Lillian asked him to book her flight he was more than happy to do so. Since there are many miles between Kentucky and California, they knew that when the opportunity presented itself, they needed to visit Ellis who had been ill. Dudley, his older brother had passed years earlier and all of John and Hattie's offspring stayed in contact with each other. Shortly after their return to Louisville, Ellis passed away. His daughter, Mary Thelma Whitlock McCall understood the expensive cost of flying and understood why they all could not return to attend his funeral. Charles D. and Solomon kept in close contact with each other especially since Solomon lived just one block away on Gallagher Street. Charles D. was always happy to see 'Sol' stop by the flower shop. They would enjoy each other's company laughing about the old times. Sol also loved to talk about his grandson he called 'Red' who was a star football and basketball player at Central High School. Since 'Sol' was skilled in landscaping and horticulture, Charles D. was constantly referring his name to businesses that needed landscaping for beautification of their property. He and 'Sol' also laughed about the different jokes played on co-workers at the post office where they both had worked.

As time moved on, Charles D. and Parthenia's grandson Leon Jr. graduated from Louisville Male High School in 1962. After he attended Indiana University Southeast in Jeffersonville, IN, for about three semesters, Leon decided to transfer his credits to Western Kentucky University located in Bowling Green, KY. In 1960, Charles D. taught Leon Jr. how to drive a car and he obtained his driver's license after successfully demonstrating to the county police officer that he was indeed a safe driver at the age of 16. Since Charles D. knew Leon had delivered many of his designs and collected from his clients, he knew it was time to accept Leon's yearning to obtain a degree in Political Science. Leon had successfully mastered two years of the German language while at Male High School. He had excelled in math and physics as well. It was time to allow Leon Jr. to achieve his goals.

Even though Charles D. and Parthenia had grown very fond of having Leon Jr. live with them, Charles D. knew Charlene had asked him when she was twelve years old and a Girl Scout to teach her how to design baskets, casket sprays and many other types of floral arrangements. It was at that time Charles D. allowed Charlene to interview him and begin recording many names of his 'Whitlock' family members to include his paternal grandfather, a Caucasian and famous medical doctor who set up in practice in Hopkinsville, KY. After Charles. D taught Charlene to design floral arrangements, she began using vast amounts of ribbons to accentuate the designs. He received numerous compliments on her ideas. Once Charlene turned sixteen, she was given a few driving lessons by her mother, Thelma, who also paid for summer driving class through the Jefferson County Public Schools when Charlene attended Western High School on Rockford Lane. Charlene quickly passed her written and driving exams. Charles D. could depend on his family members like Charlene and Thelma to come home from school and help with his floral business. After Charles D. retired in 1962 from working 35 years at the U.S. post office on Broadway, he was aware that he now had a lot of time for his business. He used those hours from working the second shift at the post office. With the help from Mollie Bennett assisting with the household chores on the weekends, Charles D. was happy to be able to pay all of his family members for their own services. Charlene and Leon Jr. had no reason to play 'Robbing Gramps' anymore. Charles D. truly taught them to earn their own money while working for him in his floral business. When Charles D. and Parthenia wanted to pay Thelma, she would ask her mother to take the money, place it in an envelope, and put it safely in the corner of Parthenia's china cabinet for Mildred, her sister to receive on her next visit. Thelma realized the stress that Mildred was under moving from city to city, state-to-state along with her children having to change schools constantly. Mildred filled out applications for numerous nursing positions as well as sat in the pews of her husband's churches or sat on the organ bench playing beautiful hymns for his churches. Thelma realized life for her sister was not all peaches and cream. Many times when Mildred called to speak to Parthenia and Charles D.'s home at 1611 W. St. Catherine Street, Thelma was there too but always told Mildred to talk to their parents but call her collect that night at her own house. The two sisters communicated like this for years to come.

Chapter 18

During the 1960's, Mildred moved from Cape Girardeau, Missouri to Atlanta, Georgia, to Tyler, Texas, where she continued nursing at various hospitals playing the organ at the various churches where her husband, Rev. David F. Harris was appointed by the bishop of his district of the A.M.E. churches. When their oldest child, Parthenia, graduated from high school, she made history as being the first African American to graduate from John Tyler High School. Parthenia, Charles D., and Thelma managed to save enough money for transportation to be there at her shining moment. After they hugged Davida, Thelma Louise, and David, Jr., the next day they returned to Louisville, KY. Charles D. had his floral business on his mind. After Charles D., Parthenia, and Thelma returned to Louisville, they discussed the fact that Charles D. and Parthenia had never applied for their Social Security benefits. They had lived off the amount of money Charles D. received from his retirement from the 35 years of working at the post office. He received only a moderate income from the floral business. Parthenia had worked very little outside their home, but she had put in plenty of hours in the floral business. Thelma drove them to the Social Security office and after researching their work records, they were able to receive their Social Security checks. Charles D. could hardly wait to take his elderly stepmother, Miss Melissa, to the

Social Security office for her to apply for her monthly checks. Each of her five children had offered their mother the opportunity to live with them. They were all kind to their mother. Charles D. also shared some of his Social Security back pay with Miss Melissa.

Later that spring, Charles D. and Parthenia counted their stack of one-dollar bills and their stack of ten-dollar bills they kept hidden in a spot in their home. They asked Thelma if she would be willing to add them to her very busy schedule and help get their reservations to make their first trip abroad to the Holy Land. They recalled the days when Thelma helped drive them to attend the Billy Graham Crusade in Louisville, KY in the 1960's. They loved to hear George Beverly Shea sing the song, "I Walked Today Where Jesus Walked." They also loved to hear him sing, the song, "The Love of God." Charles D. and Parthenia made the statement that until all of our churches and people of all skin colors begin to show their love for God through the integration of worship in this country, the United States would not be fully integrated. After Charles D. and Parthenia shared the news with her sister Mollie Bennett, she eagerly went home to count her dollars and asked Thelma to make her reservations as well to accompany her sister and brother-in-law. Since Mollie had been with Parthenia through her stroke and walked over to her home back and forth even at night in darkness, they were more than happy for her to accompany them on this grand trip. Mollie had walked in the dark to catch the city bus to ride to J.B. Atkinson School to work in the lunchroom. She along with other cooks prepared meals for the students and school staff. There were no microwave ovens around. Just robust women who had the strength and desire to lift heavy pots of food such as baked turkeys, hams, soups of all kinds as well as vegetables. All of the family knew Aunt Mollie wore used clothing. She got them from her well-to-do employers, where she worked out in service, who gave to her after she worked on bended knees scrubbing their floors. Everyone knew Aunt Mollie had shared her weekends off from the school lunchroom to work in Charles D. and Parthenia's home. Whether watering plants outside that were for sale or sweeping or vacuuming their floors, they wanted to see Aunt Mollie enjoy herself on this grand trip. Leon Jr. was thrilled that Aunt Mollie got the chance to travel with Charles D. and Parthenia. Charles D. and Parthenia allowed Leon Jr. to drive Aunt Mollie to J. B. Atkinson School before he reported to Louisville Male High School for classes. Leon Jr. only had to drive two blocks to her home to drive her into the Portland area of town to her job and return Charles D.'s car home safely. Aunt Mollie was the cake baker in the family! All of Parthenia and Charles D.'s family members loved to eat her hand-whipped cakes. Even her youngest sister, Laura's children and grandchildren loved her cakes and were eager to see Aunt Mollie get this opportunity to travel to the Holy Land.

It was only a few years after Charles D. and Parthenia returned home from that trip abroad that Charlene, their oldest granddaughter had been accepted into a nursing program to become an R.N. at Western Kentucky University, the same state college where her brother was attending. She returned home after attending one full year. Charlene told her parents that her instructor became upset with her after she asked if some of her friends who also enrolled in the same state college could be accepted into the nursing program. Charlene was told by the nursing director that because she graduated from Louisville Male High School it was one of the reasons she was allowed to enroll in her nursing program as their first single female of color. The director stated that her friends, who graduated from Central High School, could not enter into her nursing program. The instructor told Charlene that she would rather take a Male High or Manual High School 'C' before she would accept a Central High School 'A'. Charlene thought to herself, how dare that nursing director insult her own mother's alma mater, when her mom, a 1935 Central High School graduate, had obtained her master's degree in 1962, and her Bachelors in Public School Instruction in 1939. Charlene did ask her instructor if she had obtained her master's degree from Indiana University as her own mother had done by studying and making the necessary grades. The answer was no along with the threat that Charlene would not be coming back to their nursing program after the spring semester ended. Charlene told her parents that she would work, save her money, and maybe one day she would return to another nursing school that did not reveal such hatred toward people of color.

After Charlene enrolled and attended a business school inside of the Speed Building located on Guthrie Street in downtown Louisville, she decided to marry a young man from Breckinridge County whom she had met in 1965. After dating for over a year, Charlene and Chester F. Holloway married on February 4, 1967. Attending their wedding were: Leon H. and Thelma Whitlock Hampton, Leon H. Hampton, Jr., Charles D. and Parthenia Whitlock, Mollie Bennett, Laura Bennett, Ed and Louise Ballentine, Mildred N. Harris, Parthenia Harris, Dorothy Letcher and Bobbie Jean Holloway. Performing their ceremony was the Rev. Dr. Emmanuel McCall, pastor of Twenty-Eighth Street Baptist Church. Charlene received a beautiful bouquet of flowers to hold in her hand from none other but Charles D. Whitlock, her own maternal grandfather, the florist.

Thelma had decided to resign from playing for over 25 years at the Mount Lebanon Baptist Church. She had served as the minister of music, having taught numerous children to play the piano, organ and other instruments for the morning, evening and night services as well as Sunday school and Vacation Bible school. Thelma had been very faithful to play for many funerals and special programs. For years Thelma had laughed about how Rev. Dr. Floyd Lacey, a student at the Southern Baptist Theological Seminary, came to her one Sunday after church services requesting that she provide the music at his wedding to Elizabeth Ann Jackmon. She quickly agreed and on June 20, 1964, Rev. Lacey and Elizabeth became one.

Thelma was called and was asked if she would be the minister of music at Centennial Olivet Baptist Church on Oak Street in the California Neighborhood. She agreed and was happy to have her own Aunt Lillian Brooks (oldest sister of Charles D.) singing in the senior choir. Thelma always had a close cousin-relationship with her Aunt Lillian's daughter who was nicknamed 'Little Lillian'. 'Little Lillian' had visited Thelma and Leon at their home at 1037 So. 17th Street many times. Leon Sr. would assist her husband, Clarence Kelly, when he was attempting to assemble bicycles he had purchased for his children. 'Little Lillian' even asked Thelma to give her a few driving lessons. Many people knew Thelma taught several of her close friends to drive such as Mary Prince who had moved to Louisville from Hopkinsville, KY and had joined the Mt. Lebanon Baptist Church. Mary Price would also welcome her niece, Mary Louise Herring to visit her so that Mary Louise and Charlene could spend time with each other as well as attend church together in the summer time. Thelma also taught her friend, Anna Elizabeth Medlock to drive.

After a new minister was called to preach at Centennial from a different city and state, Thelma agreed to step aside so that he could enjoy the type of music he appreciated. Thelma had played for numerous services at several churches, organizations, and functions within the city and state. It would not be long before her phone was ringing again with requests by another minister inviting her to share her musical talents.

In 1966, Leon Jr. graduated from Western Kentucky University obtaining his degree in Political Science. Charles D. and Parthenia wanted him to live with them again, but he chose to move in his own apartment near the University of Louisville where he enrolled into the Brandeis School of Law. His grandparents were quite proud of how he worked for different mayors such a Kenny Schmeid and William O. Cowger. After he began working for the County Judge Executive, Marlow Cook, who won the senatorial election to become a Kentucky United States Senator, Leon accepted Senator Marlow Cook's offer to work in his office as a Congressional Aide. He knew he could get an apartment through the contacts and assistance from Ms. Dora Jean Lewis from Louisville, KY. Leon quickly packed his bags and bid everyone a farewell. Parthenia cried as he left for Washington, D.C. Before Leon Jr. left for D.C., he assisted his sister, Charlene, in finding a job at the now defunct Louisville Trust Company Bank as the first black female bank teller to wait on all customers. Leon enjoyed stopping by the bank to speak to his friend, Gordon Guess, as well as seeing his sister working. While in training she also had the opportunity to provide services to the Louisville television personality, Diane Sawyer's mother when Charlene worked at the Hikes Point branch on Taylorsville Road.

Leon Jr. kept in close contact with his grandparents and parents. Parthenia would be glad to inform Thelma when he called her home. Since the Vietnam War had begun, many men were being drafted. Leon Jr. received his notice and left his job in D.C. Showing up at Ft. Knox, Kentucky only to meet a young man by the name of Jerry Abramson. After their basic training, Leon Jr. received the "American Spirit Honor Award" which was the highest award presented at the end of their basic training. My, how Charles D., Parthenia, Leon Sr., Thelma, and Charlene beamed with pride. The awards ceremony was shown on a local Louisville television station. Charlene called her parents and grandparents that evening so that they could turn on the local television station to watch their family member receive his award.

After Leon served his two years in the U.S. Army, he returned to Washington, D.C. to work in the office of Kentucky Senator, Marlow Cook. Leon developed a close bond with the senator, his wife, Nancy, as well as their five children. Leon enrolled in American University Washington College of Law where he would receive his juris degree after working in the KY U.S. senate office in the daytime and attending law school at night. He made all of his family very proud of his accomplishments. He also phoned his family members asking them not to try to spend money to come to his graduation.

Chapter 19

The very next year Charles D., Parthenia, and Mollie traveled to the Holy Land. It was time for Davida, the second daughter of Mildred and Rev. David Harris to graduate from John Tyler High School in Tyler, Texas. Even though her parents had moved to Temple, Texas, where Rev. David F. Harris had been assigned to another A.M.E. church, Davida requested to live with a true family friend who allowed her the opportunity to graduate from the school where she had made many friends. She was one of only two Black students who sang in the school's a cappella choir. Davida was happy to look out into the audience and see her maternal grandparents and Auntie Thelma sitting with both of her parents and siblings applauding, when her name was called to receive her diploma.

Within the next two years, Mildred and David F. Harris began having marital differences. Charles D. and Parthenia's home, with the florist shop addition, located on St. Catherine Street was razed after Urban Renewal bought the entire block. They moved into a home big enough for Mildred to come live with them if she chose to do so. There was no iron fence or gate at 1848 Date Street just like the one on St. Catherine Street. Mildred decided to leave Texas and enroll in Wilberforce College in Ohio. Two of her daughters, Parthenia and Davida, enrolled as well. After attending two semesters, Davida decided to leave and enroll into Homer G. Phillips

School of Nursing where her mother had graduated and been able to gain employment in each and every city where she had moved with her family. Parthenia, Mildred's oldest daughter, decided to leave Wilberforce and began dating a young man. After Parthenia saw how well her younger sister was managing in nursing school, she decided to enroll as well. Charles D. and Parthenia were eager to assist in any way that they could along with Auntie Thelma. They all would write letters of encouragement and send them spending money as often as possible. When they were on a break from their classes, their grandparents would send for them to come visit and provide delicious meals. Gramps would always make his famous "lo-blobby" for them and laughed when they seemed to want to finish their meals in a hurry. The "lob-lobby" consisted of cornbread, butter, and molasses that he mixed up together on his plate and he would eat the entire mixture. After three semesters later, Davida's mother, maternal grandparents, Auntie Thelma and younger siblings of Davida sat in the audience while Davida marched in graduating and leading her older sister's class to cheer them on to their graduation date. This was an event that the grandparents would talk about until their dying days. Parthenia graduated in 1973 and once again Charles D., Parthenia, and Auntie Thelma showed up to sit with her sister Mildred who was grinning from ear to ear about her older daughter's graduation to become a registered nurse just like her. Charles D. and Parthenia were very proud of their daughter Mildred's efforts to encourage her daughters to further their education. They called Mildred and stated that Thelma and her friend Anna Medlock were going to the Holy Land. Before Thelma could leave town, she was viciously attacked after walking out of a bank at 18th and Dixie Highway. She was robbed of her purse that possessed not only some of her spending money but her passport. It was the first week of December and she knew that it would take another six weeks to obtain another passport for her to travel to the Holy Land, which was in about two weeks. Someone called two days later and stated that her purse had been found in a dumpster. There was no money, not one of her credit cards, but her passport was found. After reporting to the police that her purse had been found, she quickly reported that the credit cards were still missing. She was able to visit the Holy Land with Anna as she had planned. Upon her return, Charles D. and Parthenia informed Thelma that they were going to the Holy Land again, but this time they had invited Mildred to go along with them. Charles D. was surely trying to make amends for all of those beatings. When they all returned from their trip, Charles D.'s old station wagon stopped running. Thelma started thinking about all of the sacrifices her parents made for her to attend Indiana University and wanted to return some of the favors someway. She bought her parents a brand new station wagon from Bill Young, her salesman. Surely, her parents had made quite an impression on her about sharing whatever she had. Thelma bought herself a used car which she proudly drove to and from work.

Charles D. and Parthenia had spoken so highly of his second granddaughter's accomplishments that it would not be long before his oldest granddaughter, Charlene, would enter Jefferson Community College of Nursing. Before Charlene could enter her last semester, Parthenia suffered another massive stroke on December 30, 1974. After hospitalization for three weeks, Parthenia was discharged and able to return home. Once again, Mildred would come to provide her highly skilled nursing services, but the stroke caused Parthenia to lose her hearing. She also suffered from the loss of her peripheral vision. When Leon Jr. would call from Washington, D.C. family members would print notes on chalkboards so Parthenia would know what he had said to her. It was pertinent that everyone stood directly in front of her in order for her to see them. Even Becky, her 7-year old great-granddaughter was aware of that need.

Charles D. had decided that Parthenia would not be placed in a care home, but wanted to care for his 'Pal' himself. He did accept help from Parthenia's sisters, Mollie and Louise, when they were available. Even though he knew both of his daughters worked, they were available whenever he called them. Thelma continued to teach school and had been assigned to Engelhard Elementary School as she still continued to give private piano lessons and assisted Charles D. with his floral business. Thelma also developed a long-time friendship with one particular teacher named Johanna Hounchell. They both were very good friends with Mrs. Dorothy Burns, also a schoolteacher at Engelhard.

Charles D. was delighted when Charlene came for a visit with her two daughters, Becky and Bonnie, with her infant son, Christian Stephan Holloway born December 20, 1974, during her semester break while in nursing school. This always seemed to lift up their spirits. By then there were four great-grandchildren. Young married Parthenia Johnson had given birth to a son, Vernon Johnson, III, whom she brought to Louisville whenever she could. Her visits always delighted Parthenia and Charles D.

Chapter 20

Even with some of the best care that could be given to a massive stroke victim at any hospital in the city of Louisville in that era, it could not prevent Parthenia's passing. After Charles D. agreed for the nursing staff to provide life support to his wife of almost 59 years, it was time to accept the challenge of letting his 'Pal' be called on to glory. When Mildred arrived from St. Louis, Missouri, she asked that the life support be stopped to allow her mother to die in peace and dignity on March 7, 1975.

The multitude of floral designs filled the entire circular walls of the Mt. Lebanon Baptist Church. Many family friends and church members, as well as business patrons throughout the Louisville community, filled the pews of the church. Choirs from other churches where Thelma had played joined in and sang songs of tribute to the memory of a kind, unselfish, devoted wife, mother, grandmother, great-grandmother, sister, and Christian. At the graveside service, Thelma Louise Harris' taxi pulled up just in time for her to be with her mother, Mildred, Auntie Thelma, 'Gramps', siblings cousins and other family members.

The weeks went by and Charles D. quickly purchased a headstone for the double lot he bought in Greenwood Cemetery on Hale Avenue. He and Parthenia had decided years before to be buried where her parents and many other family members and friends had been laid to rest.

On May 9, 1975, Charles D., Leon H. Hampton, Sr., Thelma W. Hampton, Mildred N. Harris, Thelma Louise along with Chester Holloway and he and Charlene's three children witnessed Charlene receiving her associate degree from JCC's Nursing program. The graduation exercises were held on the Belvedere located not far from the Ohio Riverfront where Charles D. had taken Parthenia, Leon Jr., and Charlene to go fishing as well as to the back door of some restaurants to purchase food in the decade before. Charlene's entire family knew things had changed for the better here in Louisville, KY.

The next month Charles D., Thelma W. Hampton, Mollie Bennett, Charlene, her two daughters and infant son witnessed Thelma Louise Harris' graduation from high school in St. Louis, Missouri.

Thelma W. Hampton continued to give piano lessons, play at churches, for numerous weddings, anniversaries, various organizations, church conferences city or statewide. She always found time to assist Charles D. in his business as well as write to Mildred, her sister. Mildred had applied to work as a nurse at the post office in St. Louis and was hired after Charles D. made two phone calls regarding his previous employment at the U.S. post office for 35 years. He simply asked that his highly skilled nurse-daughter be interviewed for gainful employment.

Just about one year after Parthenia's death, Charles D. and Thelma W. Hampton received an urgent call from the late Parthenia's Aunt Lavada Martin. She stated that she was acutely ill. She asked that they come at once to see about her condition. Mildred was summoned and flew into New York City. Charles D. and Mollie Bennett rode in the car Thelma W. Hampton rented and drove to New York City. After assessing Aunt Lavada's health condition, all family members were in total agreement that she was well enough to travel to Louisville in the same rental car that Thelma had driven to New York City. Aunt Lavada's blood pressure was within normal limits at the age of 87 years, she was not on any prescribed medications, and took vitamins due to encouragement by her medical doctor. One wonders if she was simply lonely for family members.

After two years passed, Aunt Lavada Martin continued to live under the roof of Charles D. Each night this gentleman in his late seventies would pull his couch out into a bed in his living room so that Aunt Lavada could continue using the bedroom he had shared with his 'Pal', Parthenia, Lavada's niece. In 1980, Thelma Louise graduated from Homer G. Phillips School of Nursing that had been renamed St. Louis Municipal School of Nursing. Also, that summer Charles D. informed his physician of the pain in the left lower quadrant of his lower pelvic area only to find out that he had developed a hernia from pulling out that couch in his living room each night. Even though Charles D. had survived several heart attacks over the past nine years, his cardiac physician, Dr. Post, gave the okay for him to have a simple hernia repair. When his daughters Thelma and Mildred were informed, they told Charlene who encouraged them not to cancel their trip by train to California to join Thelma Hampton's Central High School Class celebration. They were hoping to visit with the late Rev. Hollis Bell's sisters and visit the church where Thelma's classmate, Rev. Sneedy Foust was pastoring. Charlene visited Charles D. in the local hospital as well as Johanna Hounchell-Camenisch who was stopped by the nursing staff before she entered his ICU room. Johanna simply let them know that she was his daughter and needed to check on her father. Even in 1980, there were long stares given to this Caucasian woman visiting an African American father.

On a Saturday morning after Charlene left the hospital at 7:02 a.m. from where she was employed, she picked up Aunt Mollie Bennett at her home at 1546 Gallagher and after arriving at 1848 Date Street witnessed several of their male cousins removing Aunt Lavada Martin's furniture from Charles D.'s house. No one had been informed that she had planned to move to Clarksville, Tennessee, where she was born. Charlene and Aunt Mollie Bennett had begun designing floral arrangements. Charlene had agreed to deliver them while Aunt Mollie answered the phone to take more orders. No one had wanted to burden Aunt Lavada with either of those tasks. It was Charles D. who had taken her to the market when she needed to go and he agreed to allow her to stay there for free. She insisted that he eat the food she cooked on his stove in his house. He even gave her the money to buy most of the food. Charlene and Aunt Mollie spoke to Weldon, James Keesee, and their friends who had driven to Louisville to assist Aunt Lavada in moving to Clarksville, Tennessee. Everyone said their goodbyes. That evening when Charlene went back to the ICU to visit Charles D. he told her how cold his feet were and she simply took off her warm socks and placed them on his feet. Charlene's feet had grown to a large size but not as large as Charles D.'s. She also mentioned to him the fact that Aunt Lavada Martin had moved away earlier that day. He only chuckled and grinned with delight. He stated he was happy to get back into his own bed and bedroom.

When Thelma and Mildred called to Charlene's house, she informed them of the news about Aunt Lavada moving. Their laugh could be heard for a while. After Charles D. was discharged from the hospital to Charlene's care, a day or so passed and his daughters Thelma and Mildred returned from their California trip. Mildred quickly returned to St. Louis. Thelma kept playing the piano or organ at Antioch Baptist Church at 17th & Dumesnil Streets. She continued to play for Vacation Bible School, Sunday morning services, revivals, as well as some evening services. When the school year started she also kept giving piano lessons on Saturdays and after schools hours during the week.

After Charles D.'s older brother Solomon passed away, he stated to Charlene that he never feared death. In fact, he stated that he had dreams of his late 'Pal', Parthenia, coming to him in a white robe. As Charles D. began to experience a decline in his health, he accepted the fact that he needed to have a pacemaker inserted in his chest. Thelma was scheduled to be at another hospital with Aunt Mollie Bennett on the same day. Charlene asked her 11-7 shift supervisor, Evelyn Wulf, R.N., if she could leave early the morning of his procedure. After getting the okay, Charlene waited patiently in the waiting room until she could see Charles D. The next day, she and Thelma together brought him home. Due to the fact that his condition of heart disease was advanced, Charles D.'s feet and ankles began to swell, but he never complained. On April 26, 1981, Charles D. and Charlene celebrated another birthday with family members.

On May 4, 1981, when Thelma went to check on her father, she found him peacefully lying on the floor of his floral workshop. There sat a lovely basket of flowers that he had just designed.

Again, there were multitudes of floral designs that encircled the walls of Mt. Lebanon Baptist Church for the very first African American florist in the city of Louisville and the entire state of Kentucky. The flowers were to express sympathy to a family that would surely miss his history of giving of whatever money he had as well as sharing of his poetry and love of life itself. Thelma had been so kind to pay some of Charles D's. bills. At age 83, Charles D. had allowed his floral business to become an expensive hobby. After the sale of Charles D.'s home, Thelma and Mildred agreed to give all of the names of Charles D.'s preferred customers to Judy and Sam Watkins, former neighbors of the Hamptons. All six of his grandchildren and four great-grandchildren would miss 'Gramps'. Leon Jr. would stand tall in front of the congregation during the home going services and read an astounding tribute from him and Charlene.

Thelma continued playing the piano for churches, giving piano lessons in her home as well as requesting different churches to allow her piano students to perform at recitals. These recitals gave their interested parents, grandparents, siblings, and friends an opportunity to congratulate the piano students and encourage them to use their talents as long as they possibly could.

A few months after Charles D.'s death, Thelma and her husband, Leon Sr., were informed by Charlene that Leon Jr.'s doctor told her the results of the biopsy. Leon Jr. had been diagnosed with Hodgkin's disease, a cancer of the lymph nodes. Even though Thelma had been thinking about retiring from teaching school in the Jefferson County Public School system, she decided that she would take a leave of absence to be with her son at the National Institute of Health in Bethesda, Maryland. Thelma drove Leon Jr.'s car back and forth from his residence in Alexandria, Virginia, driving on the Capital Beltway as though she had been driving it for years. While Thelma was with Leon Jr., Charlene stayed in Louisville, KY, caring for Leon Sr. who had minor surgery. In about two weeks Charlene canceled her family vacation, flew into Washington, D.C. enroute to Alexandria,

Virginia, to relieve Thelma of her duties and allow Thelma to return to Louisville to be with Leon Sr., her spouse. Charlene returned to Louisville 10 days later.

Leon Jr. accepted his chemotherapy and after six months of treatment he returned to work and was informed that he was cured. He stated to his father, Leon Sr. that he could feel the prayers come from across the miles from all of the members of Mt. Lebanon Baptist Church where Leon Sr. had asked the entire church to pray for his son's recovery.

Whitlock's Compositions

My Mother

It takes a Mother's kindness
To forgive us when we err…
To sympathize in trouble
And bow her head in prayer…
To recognize our needs
By her loving words and deeds…
It takes a Mother's endless faith,
Her confidence and trust…
To guide us through the pitfalls
Of selfishness and lust…
And that is why in all this world
There could not be another…
Who could fulfill God's Purpose
As completely as my Mother.

By Mildred N. Harris, R.N.

Charlene Hampton Holloway, RN

Mrs. Parthenia Whitlock

Mrs. Parthenia Whitlock
What a sweetheart
What a Pal
What a helper
What a Gal
What a Mom
The best by far
That's exactly what you were.
Because of her faith, her attitude, epitomize
This is not a sad goodbye, but a cheerful so long.
See you later, so we say "auf wiedersehen"
Which is to say we'll see you again.
Lovingly, missed by the family and Charles D.

Chapter 21

Mildred continued working at the post office and kept in close contact with her three daughters who were nursing in different states. She was very proud when Thelma Louise Harris, her youngest R.N. daughter married in a backyard ceremony at the home of Mildred's oldest daughter, Parthenia. Auntie Thelma was asked to play at the ceremony and did so in a fine fashion. The close ties and relationships with Charles D. and Parthenia's children and grandchildren were remarkable. Mildred was informed by her sister, Thelma that she was officially retiring from teaching school but stated she would continue to give piano lessons in her home she shared with Leon Sr.

It was a few years later on a cold Wednesday, February 18, 1987, that Leon H. Hampton, Sr. fell backwards outside his home while throwing salt on the walkway to melt the snow. Many piano students came for their lessons on that particular weekday. It had snowed the day before. Charlene and her husband, Chet, had been shoveling Leon and Thelma's driveway. They carefully placed Leon's shovels in their own garage so Leon would not be tempted to shovel himself, since he had been diagnosed with congestive heart failure. Charlene received a call from her friend, Myra Watkins Frazier, who lived across the street from Charlene's parents. She told her that her father had taken ill and EMS was at his home. It seemed to take her forever to put on her clothes at 10:45 a.m. after awakening to the phone call. Charlene had been attempting to sleep just a few hours after working the 11-7 shift at a hospital before going to visit her dad. Upon arriving, Charlene accepted that she must let go. Her dad had died of a massive heart attack. As she pulled the blanket back from his face, she noted that he was looking up to the sky. He was truly at rest. Her husband, Chet Holloway, was by her side. Then Chet quickly left to pick Thelma up from a Jefferson County Public school where she had been hired as a substitute teacher. Upon her arrival and after viewing her husband of over 45 years she simply said to Charlene, "Well, I knew one day one of us would probably go first and Charlene we have to accept his death." Soon Jack Davidson arrived. He was their traveling friend and Thelma's walking buddy. Jack could not hold back the tears. Mayme Fitzpatrick who was another walking buddy and former California neighbor from the 1940's, called immediately. It seemed as though Thelma Whitlock Hampton had the support of not just neighbors in the Hallmark Estate, but in the entire city. Her sister, Mildred, came to be with Thelma as quick as she could board a plane bound to Louisville. Many family members came including Leon Sr.'s sister, Gladora, her two sons, Edward Tinsley, Thomas L. Tinsley, Jr. and her granddaughter, Amber Tinsley from Detroit, Michigan.

This time Mt. Lebanon Baptist Church had many floral designs but the entire circular walls were filled with Masonic brothers who had come from other cities in Kentucky to join local Masonic brothers. Three houses of orders provided some of the most cherished services that Thelma, Leon Jr., and Charlene had ever witnessed. Many friends and church members testified that they had never seen such services performed before. Leon Sr.'s family knew that he had traveled to other cities in Kentucky and provided services for other Masonic brothers. Leon Sr. had attained the status of 32nd degree Mason, but had no idea that he would receive such services. Dr. A. B. Harris mastered and oversaw all of those fine services.

Thelma had her music to keep her strong and active as well as her own faith. In the years to follow, she continued to receive calls several times a week from Leon Jr. Charlene vowed to keep the front and back lawns mowed just like Leon Sr. had proudly done at their home. Thelma talked by phone to her sister Mildred.

    Within the next year, Mildred had a severe stroke, which left her paralyzed and unable to speak. Her daughters came to her bedside. Thelma's good friend, Johanna Hounchell-Camenisch, drove her to visit Mildred in St. Louis. After Mildred received therapy at a nearby rehabilitation center, Thelma Louise, her youngest R.N. daughter took her mother to Encinitas, California, to live with her. Over the next four years, Mildred's daughters and son would visit her. Eventually, Mildred's medical condition needed twenty-four hour supervision. Her sister, Thelma came to see her as well. Thelma and Charlene began caring for Aunt Mollie Bennett in late 1992 until May 22, 1993, when she was found by Thelma one Saturday morning. She had pleasantly slept away as she had hoped in her own home. Thelma and Charlene felt they had done the best they could for a loving aunt who loved to bake cakes. They remembered how Aunt Mollie Bennett spent time caring for many family members as well as worked in the Whitlock Florist business. Aunt Mollie always appreciated being a part of the holiday dinners at Charlene's home. She was also pleased when Bonnie, Charlene's younger daughter, would eagerly drive Aunt Mollie home from church each Sunday. Mt. Lebanon and Antioch Baptist Churches were sincerely supportive again. Thelma continued playing the piano at Antioch and giving piano lessons. On February 8, 1994, while working at the Visiting Nurse Association, Charlene received a sad message from her cousin, Parthenia Mengstu, that Mildred had passed away. Parthenia loved Auntie Thelma so much that she felt it may be too painful to call her at home and inform Thelma of her sister's passing. Charlene was excused from work and informed Thelma of her only sibling's passing. Thelma stated she felt that she had done the best she could do to help her sister. This strong woman of God, who had suffered many close losses, quietly grieved to herself. Mildred's corpse was flown to Louisville to be buried in the city where she was born. Antioch's choir provided beautiful music as the pastor presented a beautiful eulogy to a fine R.N., loving mother, sister, grandmother, niece, aunt and cousin. Many members of Mt. Lebanon came to the visitation to offer condolences as well as many local cousins. There were even cousins who drove from other states to be with family. For sure Mildred Naomi Harris, R.N. had lived a long and successful 74 years of nursing thousands of patients and even family members. Although Thelma had tried to provide piano lessons to her three grandchildren, she kept playing and giving lessons to others the month after Mildred passed. She was informed of her Aunt Lavada Martin's passing at 105 years of age in Clarksville, Tennessee, in March of 1994. It was amazing how Aunt Lavada Martin outlived all seven of her former husbands. On July 19, 1994, Thelma and Charlene both received calls from a local hospital that Aunt Louise Ballentine had passed at the age of 95 years. Thelma began to bond closely with Charlene's sister-in-law Bobbie Jean Holloway, R.N., who would pick up Thelma, Ms. Ann Calvin, and Mrs. Ona Summers. Bobbie Jean would pick them up on Fridays so they could enjoy shopping and dining at various fish restaurants. Charlene dubbed them the "Wild Bunch" but she was only kidding. These Christian women enjoyed each other's company and fellowship. It wasn't long that Thelma was about to turn 80 years old. Charlene requested that Leon Jr. join her in an attempt to surprise their loving mother with a "This is Your Life" birthday party. Many family members and friends drove and flew many miles from other states to be present. Rev. Stephen Mims provided the prayer for the food. Rev. Woodie McElvaney and Rev. Curtis Crawford gave words of appreciation of her kindness to share her musical talent at many church and civic functions. The "Wild Bunch" participated as well. Thelma continued to write letters to friends in various cities in Kentucky and other states. She occasionally traveled with the senior citizens' group at Antioch Baptist Church.

On May 7, 1998, Thelma was driving her musician friend, Cascilla Springer to a coffee concert scheduled to be held at the Kentucky Center for the Arts. A woman ran a red light and Thelma's car was totaled, but she sustained only a fractured patella (knee bone). Cascilla's back was sore. After their discharges from the emergency room of the hospital, Charlene's husband, Chet, had quickly rented a wheel chair to aid Thelma's ability to get into their home. The next day Thelma was scheduled for surgery for repair of her patella. A few days later, Charlene requested that her mother be discharged to her and informed the surgeon that she would gladly care for her mother as well as take her to physical therapy three times a week while she was on her lunch hour.

Charlene requested a leave of absence from her job to care for Thelma. After Leon Jr. came to visit them, she decided she wanted to return to her own home. Charlene visited Thelma at least three to four times per day and provided her meals. Thelma received many calls and visits from friends who wished her well. After a storm came through the area and left her block of homes without power, she decided with Charlene's encouragement to live with her daughter permanently. It made it easier for everyone. Her husband Chet said he did not mind since she and Chet had cared for his father, the late Henry Holloway, Sr., in their home the last two years of his life. Chet's father died on August 4, 1988, the day before his 89th birthday. Chet and Charlene knew they had experience in caring for elderly family members.

Charlene and Chet remembered how happy they were to have Thelma join them in May of 1992. Together they had all witnessed Becky Holloway Hogan and her sister Bonita Ellen Holloway receive their diplomas from the University of Louisville. Thelma only smiled when the tears were flowing down Charlene's cheeks. Becky and Bonnie had told their grandmother Thelma that she was the main reason that they both chose to attend and graduate from the University of Louisville where she could not enter after she graduated from Central Colored High School in the class of 1935.

Thelma quickly asked to see their large sized diplomas to have them framed in the colors of red, black and white. She played at Becky's wedding in 1991 at Mt. Lebanon Baptist Church and agreed to play for Bonnie's wedding June 19, 1993 at Mt. Lebanon Baptist Church. Thelma was happy to attend the high school graduation of her only grandson, Christian S. Holloway in May, 1992. He too followed the footsteps of his Uncle

Leon H. Hampton, Jr., mother, Charlene Hampton Holloway, and two sisters when he graduated from Louisville Male High School. Christian could hardly wait to enter the University of Louisville when the fall semester began.

Chapter 22

Leon Jr. requested that Thelma come to Washington, D.C. to witness the unveiling of the nationally-known sculptor from Louisville, Kentucky, Ed Hamilton. Several of Thelma's close friends were going as well. In fact Johanna Camenisch was going to meet Thelma in D.C. After Charlene walked Thelma to the gate of her airline and waved goodbye, she returned to her home only to find her daughter, Becky, crying and stating that Thelma's house had caught fire. The fire caused extensive damage to her living room, music room, and the entire house suffered extensive smoke damage that had filled the basement through a hole burned into the floor. Thelma lost her piano and organ. Charlene knew Thelma had recently been closely monitored for high blood pressure by her physician, Dr. C. Ross Morrison, and she was not sure how to would tell her long distance. Leon carefully approached Thelma inquiring about the type and name of her homeowner's insurance. He gave that information to Charlene who proceeded to assist in getting all of the contacts informed. Thelma was even seen on a local television station while enjoying herself in D.C. at the unveiling. Leon decided Thelma would be told about the house fire after she returned to Louisville. After she returned and family members stopped at a fast-food restaurant, Charlene turned off the engine of her car. Becky's daughter, Jonna blurted out, "Memommy, your house caught on fire!" Becky immediately took her daughters, Janine, and Jonna inside of the restaurant. Charlene took Thelma's hand and explained that there had been a house fire the morning she left for D.C. She went on to explain that she and Leon did not want her to worry and have her blood pressure elevated. Thelma only asked, "Will you take me to see my house so I can see for myself?" She walked into the living area, saw the badly burned organ and piano, shook her head and quickly walked outside and said to Charlene, "at least I wasn't here and didn't burn up." She acknowledged to her daughter that she had lost her sense of smell. After the house was repaired, Thelma decided to give the house to Becky and her daughters. Charlene had been helping Becky with her daughters since she was teaching school at the time.

Charlene had decided to try retirement from the job of a visiting nurse on July 13, 1998. Charlene had listened intently to the sermon the day before preached at St. Stephen Baptist Church by senior pastor, Rev. Dr. Kevin W. Cosby about manna ceasing one day. Then the choir sang a song "Everything's Gonna Be Alright". Charlene stepped out on faith. She looked back over her life and decided to ask her Mom while both were living if she could have permission to write her Mom's life story to include her Mom's immediate family. The permission was granted, but Thelma asked Charlene, "Do you think anyone will read it?" Charlene placed her Mom by her side at her desk housing her computer. They would work on the book ever so often.

Thelma and Charlene began receiving many calls and requests for Thelma to play the piano or organ for various events within the city, state, and even in other states. Thelma would always reserve a few days of the first week of December to visit Leon Jr. One of her high school classmates and former Mt. Lebanon Baptist Church member began hosting luncheons and inviting about 15-20 of their mutual and professional friends who live in the D.C. area. Many graduated from Central Colored High School. She began to visit with Anna Medlock's daughter and son-in-law Roberta and Corrie Haines of Upper Marlboro, MD. Thelma continued writing letters to cousins, friends, and even playing the piano once a month at various nursing homes throughout the city and county. Her friend Roselle Merriwether began giving her a ride in her van. Thelma even played for Roselle's daughter's wedding. Thelma had given Reen piano lessons as well.

In April of 1999, one day Charlene had baked a ham, turned off her stove and asked Thelma who was lying down to ride with her to see the newest addition to the family, Maegan Charlene Helm. Charlene's younger daughter, Bonnie and husband Marcus Helm, Sr. had become proud parents of a daughter and older brother, Marcus, Jr. could hardly wait to come home from school each day to see Maegan. When Charlene and Thelma returned home, neighbors were standing outside and began telling Charlene that they thought her house was on fire. She saw smoke, but said that maybe the smoke was blowing from somewhere else. The fire department came quickly. The house sustained heavy damage due to a fire that must have started in the kitchen. The fireman noted that the stove had been burned off. Even though tears were shed, Charlene and Thelma realized their lives had been spared. Chet came home from work as quickly as possible and comforted his wife. She had begun writing chapters of a book she wanted to share with others about how her maternal grandfather, the late Charles D. Whitlock along with her grandmother, the late Parthenia Whitlock reared their two daughters. The chapters were safely tucked inside of her metal desk, which housed her first computer. Thelma had spent several days sitting beside Charlene telling her about her early life and about her pet rabbit. Charlene and Chet were blessed with another grandson through their son, Christian S. Holloway, Sr. By mid-August, Charlene was babysitting both infants, Maegan and Chris Jr., daily. Also at times taking two or three grandchildren to school and picking them up at S. Coleridge Taylor Elementary School each day. Thelma had been asked to bring her keyboard to play at birthday parties at the schools. Each day, Thelma shared her joys and memories of dear Central High School located across from S. Coleridge Taylor Elementary School.

Charlene's manuscript was placed back into her desk and received very little attention even though her mother's friend in D.C. urged her to complete her book. Dorothy Boggess completed several books about her world travels with her husband over the span of more than sixty years. One day Thelma's niece, Parthenia called and asked Auntie Thelma to play at their Dad's retirement program. Thelma quickly agreed. Thelma held no grudges against her sister Mildred's ex-husband. Rev. & Mrs. David F. Harris enjoyed her playing for his retirement services at Metropolitan A.M.E. Church in Austin, Texas, where he pastored for fourteen consecutive years. Parthenia and Thelma Louise stated that Auntie dazzled the audience when she played, 'Malotte's, *The Lord's Prayer*.'

Thelma was invited to fly to Chicago to celebrate her friend Anna Medlock's 80th birthday celebration, March 2000. The next month, Charlene accompanied Thelma to Chicago and on to Rockford, Illinois, to attend the funeral services for Anna Medlock and to be with Anna's two daughters, Roberta Haines and Giovanni Van. Thelma had always encouraged both girls to reach the highest level of education possible as their late mother had done. Both daughters requested Thelma accompany a soloist as she sang the song, "His Eye is on the Sparrow" because the young organist had never heard of that particular song. It had been Anna Medlock's favorite and her life-long friend had accepted the challenge of playing at her friend's funeral services as she had done for so many friends and family members in her seventy-four years of playing the piano. At age 83 years old, Thelma renewed her strength in God and kept to the task of playing for many events. Whether in the city of Louisville or any city in the country in the past years. Thelma has been requested to play for funeral services of cherished friends of Young's Chapel A.M.E. Church playing alongside her musician friend, Rose Montgomery, also a very talented musician. Thelma accompanied various soloists and agreed to play for the Central District Order of the Eastern Stars in the month of March 2004. She practiced the chorus called the Thelma Hampton Chorus and before the Palm Sunday services which were held at Mt. Lebanon Baptist Church (where Thelma belonged for over 70 years). She played for the Deacons Wives and the Bettie Morton Chapter's services to honor the late Katie Pearson, at Ebenezer Baptist Church on 28th Street. When Charlene arrived to take Thelma home, she quickly sat on the front pew patiently waiting while a young woman who had requested Thelma to play sang a song. This young woman knew Thelma could read notes as they were written. Charlene looked to her left and saw a young man named John Ray, also a musician, grinning and watching Thelma play the piano. She whispered to him, "Isn't my 87 year-old Mom awesome?!" He whispered back, "Yes indeed." After the young lady completed her solo and Rev. Eddie White performed the Doxology, Charlene walked over to Sister Myrna Brame, a deacon at St. Stephen Baptist Church, and offered her condolences in the loss of her maternal grandmother. The St. Stephen connection was present at Ebenezer Baptist Church.

The summer of 2004 brought about opportunities for Thelma to play for her son-in-law's Holloway-Wales-Pyles-Styles family reunion held at Masterson's and at a local park. She attended Antioch Baptist Church again that year on June 27, 2004, when Chet's family members worshiped in praise while Rev. Woodie McElvaney delivered a powerful sermon. Mrs. Nancy Falls stood up and asked the minister to please recognize Mrs. Thelma Whitlock Hampton, a former member and musician of Antioch. She and Charlene had attended the Senior Citizens luncheon in April when many people like the Rev. Wilbur Browning gave kind remarks regarding his mother. Charlene had the opportunity to do the same. Many tributes were made that day to many Christians.

The month of July was busy for all Whitlock descendants who were getting ready to join over 130 cousins, aunts, and friends for the John and Hattie Whitlock Family Reunion. Tony Scott, formerly of Louisville, Kentucky, and presently living in San Francisco, had carefully planned the reunion with his youngest sister, Rita Scott Holman. It was a two-day event to honor the descendants as well as the two matriarchs, Mary Thelma Whitlock McCall, 74 years of age, daughter of the late Ellis Whitlock, the second born child of Hattie and John Whitlock as well as Charles Thelma Whitlock Hampton, 87 years of age and older daughter of Charles D. and Parthenia Whitlock.

What a joyous occasion when family members who had not seen each other for over 20 years and family members meeting each other for the very first time gathered on July 24, 2004, in Shawnee Park. The entire family quickly stood in front of the tent that bore the sign: Proud Heritage Family Reunion—Whitlock Family Reunion.

The Whitlocks were filmed by a local television station and Thelma was interviewed about her years of being a Jefferson County Public School teacher and musician for decades. Her interview was shown on the news that evening several times as well as the next morning. When Thelma was awakened to take her blood pressure pills, she asked Charlene, "Was that yesterday in Shawnee Park?" and Charlene nodded yes.

Charlene was glad she had asked her daughter, Becky to explore the census books and microfilms at the Filson Historical Society on July 22, 2004. Becky and Pen Bogert assisted Charlene in obtaining copies of the late John Whitlock's death certificate dated March 18, 1912. With the history of Kentucky hardly issuing any death certificates for any culture from 1911 and before, Charlene was able to view her bi-racial great-grandfather's death certificate naming his own mother, Ms. Cornelia Wallis, Charles D.'s grandmother. Charles D. told Charlene about it back in 1959 when she was twelve years old and she wrote down the exact spelling. The 1900's census showed how John Whitlock, son of Dr. John C. Whitlock of Hopkinsville, KY had all the names of their children born before 1900 to the union of Hattie Morris Whitlock. The freed slave of Dr. John C. Whitlock, Ms. Cornelia Wallis, had the opportunity to live long enough to explain to little Charlie Whitlock about the complexion of his father. Charlene passed out copies at the Whitlock Reunion to family members. Rita Holman, daughter of the late Louise Whitlock Scott, told Charlene, "My late mother told me that the correct name of her paternal grandfather was old Dr. John C. Whitlock." Charlene was glad to share this information and encouraged others to go to the Filson Historical Society located at 1310 So. Third Street, Louisville, Kentucky.

Charlene understood why maybe there was a legitimate reason for the hiatus in completing her book. After she was advised by her mother, Thelma, that she should babysit her grandchildren and was reminded that it was Parthenia Whitlock who cared for she and her brother while her parents worked, Charlene was compelled to say yes. She is glad she listened to her mother. When her daughter, Bonnie had a chance to receive a promotion if she moved away to another state for little less than a year, she would need to provide any assistance. Bonnie told her Mom over the phone while she lived in Florida that she hugged her pictures of her children and husband as well, but missed them sorely. Charlene agreed to fly Bonnie's toddler and young son to Florida to visit with her after working hours. Her older daughter taught at a middle school as well as coached the girls' basketball team. Charlene could still depend on Becky to come home from work to prepare meals for her grandmother Thelma as well as her father and daughters. When everyone works together, things have a way of working out for the better. When the five-day visit was up in Florida, it was time for Bonnie to take her two children and mother to the airport, there were no tears shed. After the plane began to ascend, young Marcus began pulling the shade up and down, looking out the window as if something bothered him. Then—all at once, the tears flowed. He cried uncontrollably for about fifteen minutes. His grandmother tried to keep him calm and asked him not to make himself ill. Then she began to shed a few tears herself. For that mother-son close bond was evident and it was extremely hard not to shed a tear. Somehow, there's nothing like a 'Mother's Love'.

Charlene knows about that mother's love from having heard her mother play songs at home such as, "It Pays to Serve Jesus Each Day." Then she may go on to play, "My Hope is Built on Nothing Less than Jesus' Blood and Righteousness" and on to play, "My Tribute." Oh, it was a happy day when Charlene witnessed alongside Thelma, Marcus Helm, Jr. and Jonna Hogan being baptized by the Rev. Jerome Brown at St. Stephen Baptist Church. Charlene was happy when Bonnie announced after returning from her job assignment in another state that she did get the promotion. No wonder Charlene loves the song, "If I Can Help Somebody As I Pass Along, Then My Living Shall Not be in Vain." Charlene loves another song, "If It Had Not Been for the Lord on my Side, Where Would I Be?" She also remembers how Charles D. and Parthenia cried when she and Leon confessed their love of God. What sweet memories!

Now the next task for Thelma, Charlene, and Rose Montgomery was to prepare to play for Thelma's grandson's wedding on September 25, 2004, at Quinn Chapel A.M.E. Church on Muhammad Ali Blvd. Charlene knows her job about getting everyone lined up for practices. She knows that each morning when she arises and peeks in on Thelma it's time to quickly pray to the Almighty Father for last night's lying down and this morning's arising. When this nation has been on high level of alert, one should know you don't have to be in other countries defending your country and other allies' rights against terrorism when it has shown its ugly face in our own country. One knows we can be here one moment and gone the next. There is no specific age when the last breath leaves our body.

In the meantime, while many brides, grooms, and family members prepare for weddings, Thelma is practicing the wedding march. Thanks to all of the readers of this book and the music plays on!

Bibliography

Cosby, Kevin W. D. Min "Get Off Your But!" Christopher Books, Louisville, KY 2000

Kushner, Harold S. — When Bad Things Happen To Good People, Avon Books 1981

Angelou, Maya—I Know Why the Caged Bird Sings, Random House; New York 1969

Angelou, Maya—The Heart of a Woman; Random House, Inc.; New York, N.Y. 1981

Angelou, Maya—Gather Together In My Name; Bantam Book/Published by arrangement with

Random House, Inc. New York, N.Y. 1974

Haley, Alex—Roots—Double Day plus Company, Inc.; Garden City, New York, N.Y. 1976

Walker, Alice—You Can't Keep a Good Woman Down, Harcourt-Brace Jovanovich, N.Y. 1981

Havighhurst, Robert J. Development Tasks and Education Third Edition; David McKay

Company 1973

Emma M. Talbott—The Joy and Challenge of Raising African American Children, Black Belt

Press, Montgomery, AL, 1997

Daly-Lipe, Patricia—Myth, Magic, and Metaphor, ROCKIT PRESS, U.S.A., 2005

Velasquez, Susan McNeal—Beyond Intellect, Row Your Boat Press, Laguana Beach, CA, 2007